MASTERING THE ART OF SUCCESS

Mastering the Art of Success

Robert Cabral

Writer's Showcase
New York   Lincoln   Shanghai

Mastering the Art of Success

Writer's Showcase
an imprint of iUniverse, Inc.

For information address:
iUniverse, Inc.
2021 Pine Lake Road, Suite 100
Lincoln, NE 68512
www.iuniverse.com

ISBN: 0-595-18401-4

Printed in the United States of America

For Mutti who taught me that faith in G-D
would bring me happiness and true success!

Contents

Epigraph

If you wish to attain true Victory,
Broaden your understanding of Virtue.
No one can defeat a person of superior Virtue.

Foreword

Coming to the United States, the land of opportunity, in 1970 was a dream-come-true to me. At the time I was 6 years old. My mom and I boarded a plane from Frankfurt, Germany and never turned back. In Germany I grew up in a one-bedroom apartment with my mom, my grandmother, my aunt and her daughter. My mom thought there would be more opportunity for us in the US so she decided that we move here.

It was much more trouble than opportunity for me my first few years. I was a skinny, asthma-ridden kid who spoke not a word of English. I knew nobody except my immediate family, and the only people who talked to me where those who made fun of me and played practical jokes on me. I cried many times walking home from school on those cold winter days in New Jersey. My mother told me that this would all come to pass. That one day I would tell others of these tribulations, but instead, I would have a happy ending to add. She reminded me to keep positive and to continue focusing on my goals.

I started martial art training at a very early age, mainly to keep from getting beat-up on my way to and from school. I read about the martial art masters and about their philosophies and workouts. I was enthralled with Bruce Lee, Jigoro Kano, Gichin Funakoshi and others. I also read a few years later about Arnold Schwarzenegger and how he transformed his body with visualization and hard work. These were my heroes. These were the warriors that I wanted to emulate. I didn't have many friends so I had plenty of free time to study and train. No one in my family had ever been into athletics or philosophy so I had imaginary figures that I surrounded myself with when I was alone and when I trained. Many years later I read Napoleon Hill's book "Think and Grow Rich", in it he stresses the importance of an "Imaginary Council".

Throughout the years I trained in martial arts and fitness visualizing my body and fighting abilities. I never came from a place where I wanted to hurt anyone who once hurt me; instead I wanted only to better myself. Later we moved to Florida. Adding to my studies I now began focussing on motivational speakers including the great Dr. Norman Vincent Peale and Zig Ziglar. Studying their principles gave way to more "positive attitude education". Soon I read everything I could get my hands on relating to PMA (positive mental attitude) training. I read and listened to the work of Napoleon Hill, Dale Carnegie, Steven Covey, Deepak Chopra, Harvey Mackay, Denis Waitley, Anthony Robbins, Wayne Dyer, and countless others.

I used the PMA tools to totally transform my life. From the asthma-ridden young boy with no friends I became a seventh-degree black belt (the youngest promoted under the Okinawan Karate System). Using my martial art skills and PMA I worked as a professional bodyguard to top dignitaries and Hollywood celebrities earning a six-figure income. I retired from bodyguarding and became a successful businessman with two karate schools, one in Los Angeles California, and the other in Zug Switzerland. I have succeeded in numerous business ventures due to two overwhelming reasons: faith in G-d and a dedication to a positive mental attitude.

Through the power of PMA and the skills I have learned as a warrior I have traveled the world and met some of the most interesting people. I speak three languages and have accomplished everything I have set my mind to do. I have everything that I want and have given countless people the tools to do the same.

Here in *Mastering the Art of Success*, I give these tools to you. They are simple to master and clearly laid out. Read the stories often and study the meaning behind them. Apply the techniques in your day-to-day life and make them yours.

I hope that in these pages you will find the knowledge to uncover the secret to your own success. The most important thing to remember is that when you stumble, get back up, dust yourself off and go again.

The only person who fails is the person who quits. Everyone on the track eventually arrives at his or her destination.

Introduction

You may ask yourself: What does a martial art master know about business, sales, negotiations, management and marketing?

I have worked in instructing the martial arts as self-defense, fitness and education. I have worked applying the martial arts as a professional security specialist. In the 1980's I was among the highest paid bodyguards. I have negotiated sales, acquisitions, mergers and more. What gave me the tools to tackle all of these things? Was it my ability to beat up the person I was dealing with? On the contrary. I would rarely let the person deep enough into my spirit to let them know what I did for a living, or what I had attained. I always thought that if I had to talk about it, the essence of what I stood for would be diluted. People would know they dealt with a warrior just because. The spirit was there, even if others couldn't see it, they could, in a way sense it.

Throughout my years great instructors and the knowledge of ancient warriors guided me. One of those warriors that I will refer to throughout this book is Miyamoto Musashi. Musashi was revered as the greatest warrior that ever lived. He was born in 1584. He entered and won his first duel at age 13. He said he came to understand strategy between 50 and 51 years of age. Shortly thereafter he wrote his masterpiece book "The Book of Five Rings" (Go Rin No Sho). This classic masterpiece on strategy was a modern day bestseller in Japan and is often cited as the source of Japan's success in the 20th Century. In Musashi's own words his book was not meant to be a thesis on strategy, instead he intended it as "a guide for men who want to learn strategy".

In this book I would like to extend to you some of these interpretations as well as many of my own strategies. They are for men and women alike who wish to master their own success.

First and most importantly, you must remember that success is what you make of it. The goal of this book is to bring you to a better understanding of yourself. Most of us are masters of falling short of leading. *Mastering the Art of Success* is mastering the warrior's way, mastering oneself. I would like to take the principles of this book and transcend their mere structure. I would like to delve into the what-and-how behind them and show you how to make them work for you. I have studied these principles from a warrior's point of view. For more than 20 years I have made the martial arts my life. Ever since my first fight, through my training, until my highest promotion, I have lived the warrior's life. Throughout these years I have adhered strictly to the "warriors code", every step of my life has been, and continues to be a warrior's life. Throughout this book I will reminisce about situations where I have used warriors principles to win in battles of physical nature, as well as those of a business nature. I think you will find it ironic how similar these battles are and how simple they are to win when approached strategically.

It is a warrior's mission in life to know people and to understand the terrain of what he is dealing with. A warrior studies more closely, focuses more intently and commits more fully to what he is doing. Being a warrior in the battlefield means playing with your life. The warrior in the marketplace is dealt a simpler hand; he can stand to lose one or two deals. Obviously the battlefield warrior doesn't have that luxury.

The warrior who can carry over his battlefield mentality into daily life can surely outdo his competitors *he can outdo anybody*. Approaching life as a life or death battle gives the warrior the strength to persevere in all battles. It is this, which I would like to share with you and teach you in the pages of this book. Battlefield thinking in the boardroom, marketplace or anywhere. Applying the skills and strategies of the warrior and moving you ahead of your competitors is my goal in this book.

You will hear about the following elements in the pages of this book. At times you will see the principles/elements mixed, sometimes individual. In order to help you better understand them I will break them down for you in brief detail here. They are the same principles Miyamoto Musashi used in his book The Book of Five Rings. Take each principle and associate it to its definition. See how the relationship can help you to strengthen yourself as a warrior in mastering your own success.

A synopsis of the elements:

Ground: The element of the ground relates directly to your posture, your stance. The way you are connected to the earth is the basis of everything you will do. Just like the foundation of the house is required for the strength and stability of the house, so your posture / stance will be necessary for your interaction on all levels of your life. This may, as with the foundation of the house, be the most overlooked by the untrained eye, however, without it you will surely crumble.

Water: Water is the wearing away of anything that gets in your way. Even though water may be considered among the softest of elements, it has the ability to wear away even the strongest stone. The water principle employs the strategy of constant focus, tireless persistence in achieving your goals. Water relates to your circulatory system, your blood-flow. Putting yourself in touch with this power enhances your interaction with others in that your rhythm will be fluid. People you are dealing with should be aware of the grace of your speech and the constant candor in your actions.

Fire: Fire, in its hottest sense, will deal with your emotions. Whether running white-hot or just simmering, the fire must continue to burn in each of our hearts to give us the energy to persevere. Even when times are low and the fire seems almost extinguished, we must draw in on it and add fuel to it so that it can again burn strong.

Wind: The wind relates directly to your breath. The air flowing in and out of your body is as the wind on an ocean beach. The flow of the breath is filling and replenishing the body with oxygen and nutrients necessary for life. It is an interesting fact that the body can go over a week without food, several days without water, but only 6 minutes without oxygen. Once you understand this, you will understand the power of proper breath. Your breath will relate to how you converse and interact. Your words must not become hesitated when you become nervous. Life requires a constant flow.

Void: Void is the element that I relate directly with your mind and your mind's eye (your consciousness). In essence the not knowing of things that makes them fresh and beautiful to us. The ability to see things from an un-jaded point of view. The ability to accept things that we otherwise might not be able to accept. Void is similar to the concept of Zen. Accepting that which may not be understandable. Not blind acceptance, but conscious acceptance. Dealing with the things that we must accept because they just cannot be explained. By not wasting time and energy, we can move on to larger and more meaningful endeavors.

Throughout this book you will see crossover examples of these five principles, water relating to air, fire to void, etc. The five elements and their strengths must become your tools to overcome your problems. As a master once said to me, *"I can give you the tools, the furniture you decide to make with these tools will be up to you."* I would like to offer you the same advice.

The answers to most all of your problems lie in the pages of this book. They may not be exactly worded as the specific problem you are looking to resolve. But if you read close enough and hard enough the answers will make themselves known to you. Hidden under the text is the meaning that transcends all words. If you open your mind and open your heart to the people and situations in your life, the solutions will come to you. As a warrior you must be strong yet compassionate, inquisitive yet trustful, honest and loyal. You must care enough to help and care enough to be honest. Most of all, as a warrior you must be just.

The warrior will always seek the solution that best solves the problem or issue at hand even if he may not benefit altogether from it.

I hope that by reading this book you will harness the warrior skills that lie deep within each of us and become a true warrior. But, most of all, I hope you will begin to understand the craft of the warrior. Next time you see someone performing their craft, no matter how menial it may seem to you, appreciate the care and quality with which the craftsman does it.

The stories / lessons in this book jump from topic to topic, just as life seems to follow no set pattern of logic. Often stories have similar points but different outcomes. Read and study the meanings behind the story and how it relates to you.

In the countless books I have read on strategy I have often remarked how many of the lessons / instructions seemed to fall into place with what I was already doing. If this is the case for you, congratulations, this simply means you are on the right path. Continue doing as you are doing and accept these validations humbly. If you gain only one piece of insight in how to better do something from this book, your money and time has been well spent. Use a highlighter and mark the parts of the book that make sense to you and that apply to your current place in life. Use all books as workbooks of life.

Life is a lesson to be learned and to be enjoyed.
Live, love and enjoy...

Kindest regards on your Warrior journey,

Robert Cabral

Lesson 1

Self-Empowerment

Within each of us lies the ability to achieve greatness. In you lies the same opportunity as Albert Einstein or Bill Gates. Greatness is a quality that some people develop more than others. The fact that a lot of us are shunned by temporary setbacks doesn't change the fact that the seed for greatness lies inside nonetheless. In order to accomplish what we want and become more successful, the key thing is the understanding of our potential for greatness.

Many people that we now consider great were at one time shunned for being geeks. I'm sure Einstein wasn't the hit at the local bar scene. The idea of not allowing the setbacks to influence your life will give you power. Those who are concerned with what they are trying to accomplish pay little attention to common opinion.

In order to empower yourself, you need to look at yourself. Where are you now? Each little bit of progress is an accomplishment. The first step a baby makes is as big of an accomplishment as the runner who runs a four-minute mile. If it is your goal to better yourself, you need to look at where you are starting from.

> *For a man to achieve all that is demanded of him*
> *he must first regard himself as greater than he is.*
> —*Johan Wolfgang von Goethe*

1

Greatness vs. Goodness

It has always been my opinion that it is better to be good than to be great

This is an interesting correlation because the two are really not even related. Many people relate greatness as the next step above goodness, not so. What good is greatness if it is not based on the essence of goodness? Goodness is inherently more important than greatness. I would much rather focus on becoming good than successful. Unfortunately, today's society places demands on us to be successful, famous, wealthy and powerful as opposed to good. I have much more respect for the person who supports his family, loves his wife and cares for animals than the great sports hero that may be cheating on his wife and looking out only for himself.

If we can work on being good, we can be truly successful. If we are doing the right things, we are on the track to self-empowerment. You will feel much better about yourself by helping your fellow man and moving along the ladder of virtue rather than clawing your way to the top of a mountain of liars and deceivers.

To accomplish great things we must first explore our individual ability for greatness. Understanding the idea that our greatness must be based on goodness in order to prosper, let us get on with exploring what lies deep inside of us.

> *Your eyes shall be opened,*
> *and ye shall be as gods, knowing good and evil.*
>
> —*Genesis 3:22*
>
> *Whatsoever good thing any man doeth,*
> *the same shall he receive of the Lord.*
>
> —*Ephesians 6:8*

Lesson 2

He Who Saves One Life Saves The World Entire

This saying holds a very deep message. Think about it yourself. If you can save the life of one living creature, not only have you saved that creature, but also its entire future offspring. Hundreds, possibly thousands of lives are thereby touched by your act of humanity. Think, if you do one act of kindness to one person a day, that person will pass on that kindness to everyone they see, and so on and so on. It is quite possible with one act of kindness to change the lives of a hundred people in a single day. The opposite is also true. That is, one mean word or action could affect a hundred people in a negative way. Life can have a sort of domino effect. The emotions of many people can be contaminated by a single action that you choose to take. You have an enormous responsibility when coming into contact with other people. Use this responsibility carefully and wisely.

There is so much power to affect the outcome of another's life in just a single action. One single act of kindness can go remembered for an entire lifetime. Remember your first kiss. The mind has a place where it stores positive feelings. They bring up a warm, tingly feeling inside when they are recalled. Recall them often and use that energy. These

3

"good feelings" can be spread. By spreading them to others, you, in turn, continue a positive flow in the universe.

With respect to karma, we are responsible to do acts of goodness to others. The act of goodness you bestow on someone else will eventually be brought back to you.

Each of us has a huge responsibility in this world. No matter what your current position may be, many others are depending on you. You decision to be kind or cruel can adversely affect many people. Whether you come into contact with one or 100 people today, those people will in turn come into contact with many, many more people. If a smile can brighten all of their days, a smirk can shadow the day just as well.

Keep in mind that as a human being interacting with people is an immense responsibly. Treat it as such. If you are the boss smile kindly on someone else, even if your day has been less than great. Think of how wonderful it would feel if the situation that brought you down had not occurred. You have the power to keep negativity from spreading. If you choose to smile and help the next person you are changing the destiny of negativity.

Helping this one person will therefore affect the way they treat the next person they come into contact with, and so on and so on.

A great man shows his greatness by the way he treats little men.
—*Thomas Carlyle*

Lesson 3

Relaxation Through Proper Breath

In grounding ourselves, let us also look at tools for relaxing. Relaxation comes from the principle of the element of the ground. Being calm and centered at your current place in life or your current situation allows you to deal with things in a calm rational matter. If you are not relaxed, chances are that it will show. Deep breathing is crucial. The body cannot function without adequate oxygen.

An exercise that I teach my students often is to sit or stand in a comfortable position and take ten deep breaths. Breathe in really deep, as much air as you can force into your system. Think of it flowing into your body, see it circling like a whirlwind inside of you and then immediately as it came in, expel it. Repeating this ten times will force more clean oxygen into your system then was probably there in the last 5 years. Bodies that lack proper oxygen are deplete of the nutrients that make them function. Exercising brings proper amounts of oxygen into the body. So do proper breathing exercises. I recommend that you do these breathing exercises at least once a day, everyday. You can do it when you wake up in the morning, in your car on the way to where you are going or at night before you retire to bed.

Breathing is an important preparation to make before you get nervous or anxious. It is beneficial to do these exercises if you are in a predicament, but as anything, preparation is paramount. If you are prepared then you stand a much greater chance of success. If you have not prepared yourself and find yourself getting nervous, these breathing exercises are still a valuable tool. You will notice upon becoming nervous that your breath races, as does your heart. Take the moment to concentrate on your breath, elongating it and cycling it through your entire body. Once you are in contact with your breath and your body, the nervousness will subside.

Many things can be, and are, written on proper breathing. If you have the desire to study deeper, you may consider books, tape or instruction in Yoga. But for now, learn to know your body through concentration on your breath.

Lesson 4

Posture

As an exercise rent the movie *Yojimbo*. It is a classic Japanese Samurai movie, in it you can see a great example of posture. Toshiro Mifune's walk and relaxed stance exudes confidence. He moves with candor and grace. He is a warrior and understands the movement of the warrior in battle as well as daily life.

Just as there is a proper stance in karate, there is also a proper stance in business as well as everyday life. How we stand can be offensive, defensive or balanced/healthy. Strive always for balance.

Posture is in fact the heart of grounding. How you stand, how you hold yourself, what your body language says about you makes all the difference in the world. Your stance is the precursor to battle. In understanding the stance and posture you learn how to set up your opponent. In any fight, position is everything. Relating this to business, it translates to your stance. It is your fundamental tool, use it wisely. People want to be comfortable with you. If they like you and feel comfortable with you, chances are you can convince them to buy from you, deal with you and work with you. What does your posture say to the person who stands in front of you? What does it say to the person watching from across the room?

Are you facing the person to whom you are speaking?

Is he/she crowded or pressured by you?

Is the stance comfortable to look at?

Where are your hands?

Are you maintaining eye contact with your subject?

If you face the person to whom you are speaking, there are a couple of things to remember.

First, you are not in a confrontation. If you are acting confrontational, chances are nothing will be accomplished. Do not try bullying the person into something that they have no real choice about. Nobody likes to be bullied. It is better to influence somebody by convincing them rather than forcing them.

Second, it is important to see the other person's point of view. That is why I do not sit across from people whenever possible. Sitting or standing at a slight angle allows you both to look into a similar direction and share your outlook. Try this sometime. Sit next to the person to whom you speak and angle your chair just slightly towards them. You will see there is no pressure, no apprehension, the person is placed at greater ease by doing this.

The person to whom you speak should not feel you are violating his or her space. There is nothing I dislike more than someone standing in my space. It is an uncomfortable feeling that will bring you nowhere. A good rule of thumb to remember is to shake hands with someone and then maintain that distance from him or her. In that case you are close enough to be within their circle of power, but not in violation of their space.

Your stance is one of the things that people use to judge you. Like it or not you are being judged. Examine your stance and see what it says about you. Are you slouching? Are you standing so tall that it seems like there is a pole holding you up? Your stance must appear comfortable. I try not to go into any of the rules relating to arms crossed, to the side or behind you, mainly because I find them unimportant. They are irrelevant. I have felt comfortable with people with their hands in front and uncomfortable with people with their arms next to them. The answer lies in the person. Your expression and your overall body language will clearly overcome the other things such as hand and arm position. You have to relate to the person with whom you interact. Become one with the person, relate.

Lesson 5

Eye Contact

In battle as in the quest for spirituality we understand that the eyes are the gateway to the soul.

Eye contact is important, but is often overplayed. To constantly maintain eye contact with someone is painful and quite annoying. If you've ever dealt with someone who stares at you non-stop you'll know what I mean. It can be quite annoying to deal with a person who stares at you relentlessly, just as it is also frustrating to deal with someone whose eyes wander aimlessly while you are speaking. Whether I am in battle or in the boardroom my eyes are always moving. Most often they are focused on the person I am dealing with, but I never, ever stare at them. I will examine what they are wearing, where they stand, how they stand, their hair, their clothing, and how they relate to where they are. I can get a pretty good read on a person within about 1-2 minutes. This is because I don't stare into their eyes. I seize an initial look when I shake hands with them. That is my goal. Now I can do and look as I want, occasionally glancing back into their eyes with a comfortable grin or nod. Then look around the room, look at what I'm buying or selling. Look at the surroundings, occasionally commenting on them, making the person I'm dealing with feel as thought "we're in this together". If you are relaxed, the person you are dealing with will also relax.

The posture / grounding principle is so important to all aspects of what you do that it outweighs all the others. You can do everything else in this book correctly, but if you fail in the grounding book, you will fail. It is like a house built on a weak foundation. Even though overlooked by most people, it is the most important part of the house. It is the core of the structure. The core of the structure of the body is the stance and the attitude that goes along with it. Examine this deeply and work on developing it. The foundation of a house must be poured and given time to set. The soil must be looked at, evaluated and treated.

Put a tremendous amount of work into your posture.

Lesson 6

In Relating To Others

The warrior takes immense honor in his interaction with almost every person with whom he comes into contact. Take some time and conduct an experiment. The next time you talk with someone in your day to day activities look at how you relate to them. Examine the attitude of the clerk at the store, your friends, your spouse, co-workers, etc. Don't tell them you are doing an experiment. Notice how poorly people relate to being crowded or being stared at. See how comfortably they relate to proper space. In battle it is important for the warrior to make his opponent feel as though he is relaxed. When he is relaxed, he can strike in and conquer.

In order to be at one with your opponent it is also important to be versed in the things that are important to him or her. If I know that a person I'm dealing with is very interested in fencing, I will try my best to learn a little about fencing before I meet him. How will I know that the person I will be dealing with has an interest in fencing? Good question. That comes from studying the "terrain of the enemy". This is not something you should take lightly, you must plan carefully. Remember most people do not plan to fail, they simply fail to plan. Research the person with whom you will be dealing. Ask questions of people you know that have dealt with them. Ask their secretary. Do whatever is necessary to learn what you need to know. You must carefully study what you are going into. If you were going into a battle, you wouldn't just show up on the day of battle and say, "Here I am". You would train and then strategically study what you were going into. Take this same attitude in even the littlest things.

In the days of the warriors, it was important that the warrior be trained in "the way of the pen as well as the sword." The true value of fighting can really not be seen in the fight itself. Therefore your passion about other things, everything must be as valiant as the littlest thing. It is said that if we know the littlest things, the big things are easier to understand. I try to be well versed in a variety of topics. So if I find myself in a meeting with someone whose interests are diverse, I can keep the conversation moving along. There are the rare occasions that I have met someone who had interests in subjects so eclectic that I knew nothing about them. What to do then has stumped many students of mine. Simple: Learn. This is your biggest opportunity for growth. One of the easiest ways to build a strong relationship with someone is to let them assume the role of teacher. There is nothing most people like better than to know more. Take a humble approach and learn. Ask interesting questions. Ask ask ask…

Lesson 7

The Ability To Decide

From your grounding it is important to make decisions. No one respects a person who can't make a decision. Decisions must be made quickly and followed through. The successful person makes up his mind quickly and takes a long time to change it. That is to say, he sticks to his decisions. They are not made in vein. Be sure to have your faculties about you always so that you can make a decision from a strong place at any time. Sometimes an opportunity presents itself quickly and may not reappear. You must be able to seize the moment. In a fight, the strategist looks for opportunity, it is important to see the opening and strike instantly. Then, it is important to follow that decision through. Persistence on a decision that you made makes your initial decision successful, or at least it gives it the ingredient for success. All attempts may not be met with success, but failure can be guaranteed if you don't stick to it. Obstacles must be met with fervor, don't give up. I will address this further in other chapters of this book.

Sometimes making the wrong decision is better than
making no decision at all.

The best we can do is size up the chances, calculate the risks involved, estimate our ability to deal with them, and then make our plans with confidence.

—Henry Ford

How far would Moses have gone if he had taken a poll in Egypt?

—Harry S. Truman

Lesson 8

Know Your Opponent As You Know Yourself

To be grounded implies knowing the opponent as you know yourself. Therefore it is important to know yourself. That is why I put so much stress on meditation and self-cultivation. To be familiar with yourself allows you to exude confidence without being obnoxious or self-centered. A person who is good at dealing with others is good at dealing with him or herself. Focus on your traits your habits your likes and dislikes. Find out what it is that you like and why. Also, find out what it is you don't like and why. What can you do to like these dislikes more? Why is this particular thing so important to you? What gives it that internal heat that drives you? Examine yourself from the inside out. When you come to the understanding of why certain things bother you or why they are important, you can more easily deal with them. I am in no way saying to change what you feel in your heart, but there may come a time where it is important to be able to put your personal feelings aside in order to conquer a situation.

The warrior takes his interests and relates them to the interests of the person with whom he or she deals. If you are interested in skiing and the person you are talking to is interested in weight lifting, you can discuss all the benefits that exercising has had in your life. When you relate to others look for the similarities that you both have. Talk about them and draw on them to strengthen your bond. You would be surprised how many similarities you can find with topics that are so diverse at their initial glimpse. I was a part of a conversation once between a couple of friends of mine who were discussing religion. One was a Christian, the other Jewish. They went back and forth arguing about who and which religion held the true answer. I asked if I could just interject one thing and both agreed. I asked if they could both agree on one thing… that Jesus Christ was after all a Jew. Both stopped in their tracks. I commented on how interesting the similarities were that the Last Supper was possibly a Passover Seder. I went on and on. I explained how much the Christian could learn about the root of Jesus' life by understanding the teachings of Judaism a bit more. Then I commented how the Jew could learn about the interpretation of the teachings of Jesus. Neither, after all, was asking the other to convert, they were just trying to make a point. The problem was, neither side was willing to learn anything about the others side first. After my little interjection, both sides had an interesting discussion about this topic.

All I did was open up both people's vision. I did not want to argue I wanted to add. When this fact came into the picture, the entire feel of the conversation changed. Instead of arguing see if you can't add more facts into your next conversation.

Lesson 9

Be Truly Great At Something

Success in anything you do implies being particularly masterful at the one thing you specialize in. Many people spend their lives running in circles, going from one craft to another, all the while attaining a degree of moderate proficiency in many things, yet never attaining mastery in any one. When a new student comes to me, often I ask them about their profession, their hobbies and their relationships. How much dedication and persistence a person has at any one of these is usually a good indication of how well they will fare at any new undertaking. People who flip-flop from hobby to hobby, relationship to relationship or career to career are usually not going to be particularly successful in any new endeavor they choose. They will try it for a while, then find either they succeed at it or not. If they succeed, they will stick to it long enough to see that it was easily attained and therefore not worthwhile. On the other hand if they don't get it, then their opinion shifts and they see that it is unattainable and a waste of time in their opinion. In either case they have not grown at all from their experience. Anything that is worthwhile is never easy. The lessons that you'll learn though temporary setbacks will teach you more than all the successes in the world. Also, the successes that you make without setbacks will never teach you anything about the true essence of what it is you're doing. You will come to fully understand the craft you practice by repetition and persistence.

Success takes a great deal of practice.

There is an interesting story about a man who lived in Salt Lake City quite some time ago. One day he quit his job, took his money out of the bank and went to a car show on the east coast. He bought a brand new car and parked it in his garage. At night he took the car apart, piece by piece. Then he put it back together again. Then, again he took it apart. Then, he put it back together. Each time he studied each piece very carefully. Many thought this man was crazy. He was by all means a perfectionist. This man revolutionized the car industry, even though his neighbors didn't quite understand him. Perhaps you recognize his name; Walter P. Chrysler was a perfectionist.

Grounding gives one a sense of self. With this sense of self we find little need to look outside of ourselves for unnecessary fulfillment. We are strong in body and in mind. It is crucial to be strong in both respects. Most importantly is mind. The body can relatively easily be overthrown, but the mind can stand up to immense pressure. Training the mind allows you to further your body. A mind that knows no limitations cannot be held back by physical obstacles. A strong mind is more likely to develop a healthy body, than is a strong body likely to develop a powerful mind.

> *You can't catch a tiger cub*
> *Unless you enter the tiger's den.*
>
> —*Japanese proverb*
> *There's only one way to succeed in anything, and that is to give it*
> *everything.*
> *I do, and I demand that my players do.*
>
> —*Vince Lombardi*

Lesson 10

Self Maintenance

The body is the house of the soul.

Have you ever met a person who is in an incredibly powerful position but looks like a slob? Have you wondered how they attained this position? Of course you have. Whether we like it or not we are tainted by a person's outwardly appearance. If the person is out of shape and not groomed, our opinion of him or her is swayed.

> *The temple of G-d is holy,*
> *Which temple ye are.*
>
> —*1 Corinthians 3:17*

Everything that we want others to know about us will first be judged by what they see. A program of self-maintenance is important. Do not let this *house* get run down. An ounce of prevention is worth …(you know the rest). Keep fit and keep toxins out. Everything that you eat is passed through the body before being passed out. Traces of whatever you take in stay in the body for a long time. The negative toxins affect the way you think, feel and respond. Imagine eating a heavy meal and then going for a long run. You probably wouldn't make it much past the end of the block. If you drink, your vision and coordination are impaired. Who in their right mind finds joy in impairing their own senses?

A good program of exercise will maintain the body. You will feel stronger about yourself and will be healthier. It is a fact that exercising will keep the body, mind and face youthful. You will live longer as a result. Spending an hour, three to four times a week exercising will keep your body and mind sharp. I can't stress enough the importance of tuning the body. Keep it looking good so that people will wish to look deeper to find out more about what is inside.

Early to bed, early to rise, makes a man healthy, wealthy and wise.
—Benjamin Franklin

It is only when the rich are sick that they feel the impotence of wealth.
—Charles Caleb Colton

Lesson 11

The Power Of The Mind

The power of the mind lies within grounding
just as the power of grounding lies within the mind.

He who controls his mind controls his own destiny. Whatever the mind can perceive and conceive the body can achieve. Our limitations are only what the mind puts up. Tear down your boundaries and get what you want out of life. Your mind must be sharp and precise. It remains a fact that humans use less than 10% of their mind, yet we've been able to put a man on the moon and fly faster than the speed of sound. Imagine the power that lies still untapped.

If the power of the mind would be compared to a computer it would squash even the most advanced machine. Yes, the computer can hold more information, and compute things at lighting speeds but that's where the miracles stop. A human has programmed anything a computer can do. A computer is greatly limited because the one thing it can't do is create a single thought. The computer has no emotions and no feelings. Your mind is infinitely more powerful than anything that man could invent. The greatness that lies in a single brain cell is greater than all the inventions of the last century. Anything man has created cannot compare to the feeling of love or compassion that lies deep within each of us.

The mind has the ability to love and hate, to think happy thoughts or negative ones. The power of the mind goes as far as being able to turn negative thoughts into happy ones. You can bring joy and love into your life and into the lives of others by doing one little thing, making up your mind to do so. The choice lies within you. The power to make this decision is within each of us. You will not be forced to do it. You can stop reading right now and probably make a call and change someone's feelings good or bad.

I read something in a book once that made a profound change on my life. It said that each morning when we wake up we have a simple choice to make; either we can be happy or sad, the choice is up to you. As much as possible each morning that I wake up, before I ever let my feet hit the ground I thank the Lord for the day he has given me and make the decision to be happy.

My good friend Dan Miller runs an urban country club in West Los Angeles, he is also one of the most positive people that I have ever had the pleasure of meeting. He often quotes Albert Einstein when he says, *"You can choose to look at things in two ways, one is that nothing is a miracle, the second is that everything is a miracle"*. Dan always opts for the second choice. *Me too.*

Imagine picking up the phone, out of the blue, and calling a friend to tell them how much you appreciate and love them. A simple act of kindness that could change the lives of potentially a hundred people. Why is it that so many of us say nice things about people when they are not around or worse yet dead? Why not try writing a note or a call on the phone? The law of karma can play an important role in this. Even if you are feeling un-appreciated or sad, take the first step and make up your mind to make someone else feel better.

Make everything you do special. Imagine if it were your job to announce the winning lottery ticket to a person. Imagine the energy and vitality with which you would do this. Now take that energy and put it into everything that you'll do today.

Lesson 12

Breaking The Limits

Limits are the boundaries that are placed upon ourselves by our comprehension of how things should be. For thousands of years man thought he would never fly. He looked at the stars and admired them, but he knew he could never reach them. Man admired the birds for their ability to fly into the heavens. For years and years man tried to fly but failed and failed miserably. Until two brothers came along and changed everything. Once Orville and Wilbur Wright proved that man could fly all the barriers were broken down. In a period of less than 100 years since that first flight, man made more progress in flying than he had made in the 10,000 years before that. Roger Banister shattered the limit of the 4-minute mile, 37 people broke the 4-minute mile the year after that, more than 300 the year after that. Computer speeds double every year. From my first 20 MHz machine to a multi-giga hertz machine that's out today, which will probably be a dinosaur by the time this book is in print. What similarities do these situations hold in common? Someone put enough behind their convictions to shatter pre-set beliefs. Forget what others say cannot be done. There are no limits to the ability of man.

Stop listening to other people when they say something can't be done. Whenever someone says to me "That is impossible?" I reply, "*You mean you gave up too?"* Most people do not know what I mean by that, but I hope you will. The more often somebody says, "It cannot be done" to me, the more empowered I feel. Even if I am proven wrong, which is seldom, I feel I am the better person for having tried.

Is there something that you would like to attempt that others don't believe you can do? Have people told you that you are too old to start Rollerblading—-weightlifting—karate? What is it you want to do, that you yourself believe you can do? Get up and write it down, then start formulating a plan to put that thought into action. Do it now...

> *If you are able to state a problem,*
> *Then the problem can be solved.*
> *—Edwin Land inventor of the land camera*
> *Do not look where you fell, but where you slipped.*
> *—West African saying*

Lesson 13

The Warrior Builds Allies

The fool breaks them down

The fact that there is strength in numbers is important to bear in mind. How many times have you burnt a bridge and later wish you had not? Accusations, words, and actions are impossible to take back. Consider your words and actions carefully when you interact with others. To have many people on your side will give you advantages in many areas of your life.

I count my friends as few; in fact I pride myself that I can count my good friends on my hands. But my acquaintances / allies number quite high. Everyone I meet I consider a possible ally. Every single person you meet can benefit you in one way or another; you just need to find out how. I remember a girlfriend of mine remarking once that "*everyone that is in your life serves some sort of a purpose*", a comment which I took as a very strong compliment. *I have no body in my life that is useless.* It is important to remember that I do not use my acquaintances, I merely use their skills. On the flip side, I am also there for them when they need me. We have a *useable* relationship, one that benefits both sides.

Upon meeting someone for the first time I ask questions and investigate the prospect. This is not unusual since you'll find out that people do this often without even knowing it. I examine the answers and evaluate the possibility of a relationship. I exchange business cards (very important) and generally invite the person to lunch if I feel we can benefit one another. Notice that I said one another, not me. To only benefit myself from the relationship would be selfish and would prove self-serving, this is a fatal flaw. A relationship in which only one person benefits is lopsided. Anything that benefits only one side will end quickly. People resent doing things without a trade off. I always stress to my friends, never take something for nothing. People may do it once or twice, but they will resent you. Every time someone does something for me, no matter how small, I make a sincere effort to show him or her my appreciation. Whether it is a thank you note, a small gift or a payment, anyone who goes out of their way for me knows I appreciate them. People love to be recognized for something that they have done.

By doing this I have built a network of power relations over the years. I know people in almost every field and if I don't know someone in a particular field, chances are someone I know knows someone. There is immense strength in numbers. Learn how to break down your power allies and then learn how you can benefit one another. Find out what and whom people know and be certain they know what and whom you know in turn. Offer your help to these people in your circle. Offer it freely but not free. A quaint line I always use is, "Sure I can help you, but you know you'll owe me." Delivered with a smile it always gets the message across.

Lesson 14

My Barber's Lesson To Me

I remember the first time I went to my barber Little Joe. He introduced himself to me and showed me around his shop. A close friend told me about him, so his reputation preceded him. He showed me some pictures and trinkets he had accumulated over the years. Among his prize possessions was a letter that Bruce Lee had written to him. In it, Bruce thanked and complimented him on the quality and precision with which he cut his hair and the effort he put into the styling. I was so impressed by this I did the same thing: Seeing that letter taught me so much about character and how people react to it.

Once I got home from my haircut I immediately wrote him a letter thanking him and complimenting him for his creativity and efforts. He never mentioned the letter to me, but I know he got it. We have become good friends over the years and no matter how busy he is I can always get an appointment to see him whenever I need to. I have carried this lesson over to so many aspects of my life and the person I have to thank for this is my barber Little Joe.

I also remember one of my students commenting on Michael Ovitz. She raved what a fantastic person he was. I asked her if she had ever met him, she answered no. So I asked her what it was about him that so fascinated her. She said that she set up a meeting for her boss and Mr.

Ovitz to meet. A week later Michael Ovitz sent her a personal thank you note and a small personal gift. It is these kinds of gestures that can move you to the top.

Note also that both Bruce Lee and Michael Ovitz's gestures were directed by important people toward supposedly "lower level" people. Kind gestures are important always, not only when they are directed toward someone you *need* to impress.

A warrior of the art of success understands that kind gestures are required for all people, not just those we consider important. When the top-level executives is liked by the janitor, you can surely bet he'll be liked and respected by his peers. However the person who selectively doles out his kindness to only those that will benefit him or her is insecure and in need of help.

Practice kindness to all others. Treat others as you too would like to be treated.

> *If you want to lift yourself up,*
> *Lift up someone else.*
> —*Booker T. Washington*
> *No act of kindness, no matter how small, is ever wasted.*
> —*Aesop*

Lesson 15

Fight Or Flight

There is a feeling of nervousness that is called fight or flight, or sometimes butterflies that each and every one of us experiences at some time in our lives. Whether it is the greatest fighter in the world or an entertainer facing an audience, everybody gets them. Trying to suppress them makes them come out stronger. I have always used this situation to strengthen me. Focusing on the energy, I would use the energy from this nervousness and turn it into power. It is important to know that energy is energy. What the energy does to you is the only separation that really exists. How you deal with it what either benefits you or destroys you.

I learned an important lesson that I would like to relate to you. This is a great way to overcome the nervous energy that overcomes us before a presentation or speech. In warrior skills it is the energy you face upon meeting a person that may kill you or may require you to kill them. Of course this is of a little more serious nature. Taking the presentation example into account, do the following. We'll assume you're going for a presentation before a board of executives who have it in their power to make the decision that can make or break you (in your mind).

The first thing to remember is that nothing, not any one single thing will ever make or break you in a permanent sense. Know in your heart that you can walk away from this presentation and get another one bigger and better tomorrow. This is not to say get a big head, *but be confident.* There is, after all, a reason why they are talking to you. Once you have gained some self-confidence the rest will be easier.

Breath is crucial. Most people tend to get themselves so flustered that they forget to breathe. This same thing happens to fighters. Loss of breath does many destructive things to the body and mind. Any lack of oxygen, no matter how small, will impair your senses. Your cognitive skills will suffer as a result. Take several long deep breaths. Cycle your breaths in a rhythm. Allow this rhythm to become a part of your pattern. *The breathing process must be mindless.* If it is, then it becomes one less thing to think about. That is why I have suggested in numerous places in this book to take time to sit and breathe. Practice breathing. It is the single most important function of the body that we can outwardly control.

Look around the audience, notice the people and things that surround you. If at all possible, try to have a look into the room or place you'll be before you actually begin the presentation. When surroundings are familiar, there is less chance of becoming nervous. *Remember home field advantage.* If at all possible do your presentation in a surrounding that is comfortable and well known to you.

Don't rush, take your time. A certain sign of nervousness is speaking too quickly. Examine what you say and say it slowly and with meaning. People tend to place importance on things that are said slowly. A person who rushes though his words is usually thought of as being deceptive. Breath between your thoughts. Allow the people you are speaking to time to hear what you said.

SMILE! Look someone in the eyes and smile at them. Smiling makes people think you like what you're saying, doing or selling. People generally like people who smile.

Be active. Don't stand still. *Move, move, and move.* Lift your arms, shrug your shoulders, point. Always be active. A moving target is more pleasant to the eye than one that is stagnant. But remember, move gracefully. Twitching or fidgeting is unattractive and unprofessional.

Accept the nervousness and talk about it if necessary. One thing that has worked for me in the past is putting my nervousness off on others. "Man, you guys look as nervous as I feel." Said with a smile always brings things to a different level. Or, "I can't believe you guys aren't as nervous as me, obviously you don't understand the seriousness of what your into." ***Remember humor has a great way with people.*** The easiest way to win people over is to get them to like you. Humor at ones own expense is a sure way to endear yourself to them.

To become a master of nervousness is to master life. Remember what it is that makes you nervous, make notes. If you understand what makes you nervous and then overcome it, it won't catch you again. There is an old saying in Japan associated with the great Daruma (the grand patriarch of Zen), Seven times fall down, eight times get up. Use this principle n your attempts to overcome any and all obstacles and remember the only person who fails is the one who gives up. Keep trucking and your past "failures" become lessons in how to do things right in the future.

Only those who dare to fail greatly can ever achieve greatly.
—Robert F. Kennedy

Lesson 16

Doing Nothing vs. Doing Something

There is a story that makes so much sense when it comes to the power of non-action and the power it possesses.

There were three fighters, a beginner, an intermediate and a master. All three were scheduled to fight the opposing team for the championship.

The first, the beginners stepped up to the mat, bowed and upon the referee's command began their bout. Within 5 minutes a champion was crowned.

The second, the intermediate level fight was called. The participants walked calmly to the mat, bowed, waited for the referees command and slugged it out for 15 minutes. A winner was crowned.

The third and final bout was the masters. The two men made their way to the mat, bowed and assumed the fighting posture. The referee gave the command to begin, and there was no movement. No movement from either side for 30 minutes. Both were crowned victors.

As you can see in this Koan (fable for meditation purposes), non-action holds immense power. The decision of the masters to do nothing was in fact the strongest action they could take. They understood that the first person to attack would show his weakness and thereby be defeated. Instead they decided to play on their strengths and wait. No action was their tool; victory was their prize.

In this situation the action of not doing anything was an action in and of itself. By not jumping at the gun you may be able to conquer your strongest adversary. The next time you jump up to show off your stuff, remember the story of the masters. Even if you feel you know better, wait. In the principle of non-action, the warrior holds his strengths to himself and wins thereby.

You may be accomplishing a lot by apparently not doing anything.

> *As I grow older, I pay less attention to*
> *what men say. I just watch what they do.*
> —*Andrew Carnegie*

Lesson 17

Overcoming Obstacles: The Water Principle

Any obstacle, no matter how great, lies within us.
In order to overcome the challenge in front of us,
We must first learn to overcome the obstacle within us.
The inner obstacle allows the outer to exist.

Any obstacle you have exists inside of you first. Even the ones that lay outside can be related to an internal obstacle that you have not yet met or overcome.

The most logical way to overcome outer obstacles is to first look at ourselves.

Many people I know are horrible at taking criticism. Any little thing you say to them is taken as an insult. The next time someone tells you something that you may not like, see how you react. Before you say anything take two deep breaths and listen. Then repeat to yourself what this person said. Repeat it out loud to them in a question form. Come from a calm place and ask the person if this is what they said. More than likely they may just at that point try to revoke the statement or change it. If they don't retract their statement ask them what they meant by it initially. Remember, you are coming from a learning place, don't jump on the defensive. You will use the information that you gather from this person to better yourself and thereby win.

To everything there is a season,
A time for every purpose under heaven…
A time to weep, and a time to laugh,
A time to mourn, and a time to dance.

—Ecclesiastes 3:1, 4

Lesson 18

The Kaizen System

Kaizen is the Japanese system of continuous improvement. One in which individuals and companies seek input on changes that can be made to improve functionality and success. Use this principle for your own success. Ask your friends, co-workers and employers / employees one change that you could make that would better you in their eyes. What additional service could your company provide that would bring it above all the others. If you are at the center you may not know exactly what is going on outside. If you have surrounded yourself with good people, ask their input. Of course you'll need to trust the people you ask, and you must be willing to hear the answer that is forthcoming. Listen carefully and write down your answer on a sheet of paper. Study these comments over several days and carefully evaluate their value.

If your employees are confident that adding another service or product to your portfolio would improve your business, take the advice. If they suggest striking one, listen carefully and consider the advice. If someone else employs you, it is your responsibility to bring things to the attention of your superior. Every person is responsible for the success or failure of the company. If you are not a team player, you are not a player. If you are not a good listener, you are not a good manager / leader. Make note if any improvements come up more than once, if they do, these are the ones that should get immediate attention. Ask what you can do to improve these things, ask the same person who initially brought up the point, *this is the person who may hold the solution.*

The soldiers are those who are at the front of the battle, they deal with the public, salesmen, servers, clerks and so on. These *soldiers* are as important to the battle as the generals at the command are. Good soldiers are willing to support the command; good commanders are willing to stand behind the soldiers. Recognize your place and work from there. Do not take the attitude of; "If I were the manager, I would…" This is a failure mentality. You are important to the process if you recognize your part in it. If you do not, chances are, *you are only a part of the problem.* Understand what your opinion of the solution is and contribute it. Do your part and the rest will follow.

To better yourself is to better the world that surrounds you. Take the time to better everything about yourself and the obstacles around you will perish.

Without a struggle
There is no fight.

—*Frederick Douglas*
What counts is not necessarily the size of the dog in the fight,
But the size of the fight in the dog.

—*Dwight D. Eisenhower*

Lesson 19

Learn From
The Power Of Nature

There once was this little river that ran along these rocks. The water minded it's own business and just traveled along its path. Everyday for hundreds of thousands of years the river went along its way traveling along the rocks. The rocks tried to resist, they were after all strong solid rocks. The only thing the water had going for it is that if something got in its way it could flow around it, the rocks had to stay in their place. Eventually where some of the rocks were worn down, there started to appear an indentation. Today that slight inclusion is one of the great mysteries of nature known as The Grand Canyon.

Nature is patient in its endeavors. Those who are patient in achieving their goals will one day achieve them. Haste makes waste. If your goal is worthwhile it is worth the time in preparation as well as execution.

Learn from the steps you take along the road of accomplishing your goal.
I am not bound to win, but
I am bound to be true.
I am not bound to succeed, but
I am bound to live up to what light I have.
—Abraham Lincoln

Lesson 20

Interaction vs. Counteraction

Wear down your opponent. Whether your obstacle lies in a goal you are attaining, a person you are trying to influence, or a habit you are trying to break remember the lesson of The Grand Canyon from the previous lesson. Anything that is worth doing is worth doing right. Take the time to listen to the points of view of the other side. Take for example a conversation between two people.

Situation A: John listens to Andy's point of view but whenever Andy presents a point that John doesn't like he cuts him off and says he has a better idea. He in fact is contradicting what Andy is saying and feeling. This will root Andy deeper and deeper in his point of view. As humans we are drawn closer to something that we have to defend. The more I defend my point of view on something, the more I am attached to its outcome being in my favor. By continuously telling you the plusses of my way, I need to have my way prevail in order to save face. Counteracting in negotiation distances the person you are dealing with in such a degree that you may never be ale to close the gap. Like polar opposites on a magnet, no matter how hard you try counteraction moves the sides apart without any chance of unity.

Situation B: John and Andy interact. One listens to the others point of view and asks questions about what it is that he might not agree with.

Interacting in this fashion shows Andy, John's point of view and vice-versa. The two people are now pulling each other closer and closer until they get to a place where they meet. Interaction is in essence also building a relationship. Learn this well. The relationship that is built on the interaction of negotiation bonds your opinions about your partner as well as showing you the strengths and weaknesses that you yourself may have. Instead of one business deal today, you are setting the stage for a business or personal relationship that may last a lifetime.

No matter how hard I negotiate, I never leave a negotiation if I feel that the person I dealt with collapsed under duress. The exception is if the fire principle was applied (which is very rare). I want to know that I can go back and have a friend / a partner to deal with again. Somebody who is happy to see me coming. Most people like to negotiate because it is fun. It's like verbal sparring; it's done between two friends who shake hands afterwards and continue on.

> *I know the price of success:*
> *Dedication, hard work, and an unremitting devotion*
> *To the things you want to see happen.*
> *—Frank Lloyd Wright*

Lesson 21

Making Allies Using The Water Principal

A few years ago I found myself doing an incredible amount of driving. Partially due to a busy schedule I was sometimes forced to break the speed limit. I was pulled over for speeding a couple of times. I know that this is wrong and I don't advocate that anyone should do it. However it brings me to a valuable experience that I would like to share with you.

Before I tell you I would like to explain the importance of flexibility such as the water principle. Many people find themselves stressed about one thing and then allow that stress to carry over to other areas of their lives. Instead the warrior of success should look to solve the stress from other aspects of his/her day-to-day things. The house-husband who finds himself stressed trying to get everyone ready for school and work, should enjoy the peace and quiet time when everyone first leaves for the day, take a few minutes to relax instead of immediately rushing around on the daily chores. The salesperson that could not close the sale on the first prospect should learn from the objections he/she encountered and use them to close the next lead.

I'd like to share with you an experience I had. Late one night I was pulled over for speeding. I immediately pulled over to the side of the freeway, turned on my dome light, placed both my hands on the steering wheel and waited for the officer to arrive. I knew that I had been speeding and so did the officer. As he approached my car, he asked, "Do you have any idea how fast you were going?" "I don't know exactly officer, but I was speeding, of that I am certain." There is nothing a police officer hates more than somebody who tries to make an excuse that they really weren't speeding or that there must be a mistake. For the most part, police are very well adept at pacing a speeding car. By immediately showing my hand I diffused his need for a confrontation or argument. He asked me why I was speeding. You see, now the issue wasn't that I was speeding, it was *why* I was speeding, and he was on my side. I told him the truth, I was extremely tired from working 20 hours and I just wanted to get home and get some rest. Again I apologized for breaking the law. He said "I understand, let me just ask you, have you had anything to drink?" "No I said, I am just totally exhausted, that's why I look like this." He again was on my side and had compassion for me. He sent me on my way and asked me to be more careful in the future. You see, in this whole conversation I never challenged him. I respected him for the enormous work that it is he undertakes on a daily basis. For the most part he has a very thankless job. I know this because for more than 8 years I have trained police officers in hand-to-hand combat. What they go through in emotional stress and physical risk is immense. Anyone who comes along and sincerely cares and makes their job a little easier is a welcome sight to any peace officer.

This truly was an example of the water principal in use. I needed to overcome the obstacle of getting a ticket, and the policeman had to do his job in enforcing the law. We both listened to another's point of view, and resolved the situation amicably. Police departments issue tickets in order to teach people about the rights and wrongs. Here the officer saw that his job could be done without issuing a ticket and causing negative feelings. He was right, 100%. I was ready to accept the ticket, but he was confident that I had learned my lesson, and I had.

When things go wrong,
Don't go with them

—*Anonymous*

Lesson 22

A Warrior Can Turn A Negative Into A Positive By Looking For Opportunity

I used to live a long way away from my work. It took me almost an hour to get to the office in the mornings as well as in the evening to get home. The problem was what to do with the wasted time that I spent driving. I must say, I love to learn, therefore I love to read. If I could spend two hours a day reading and educating myself I would be ecstatic. I found the perfect solution. Just down the street from my house was an audio book store. Here I could rent any one of thousands of books on tape. I would go every few days and rent several tapes for my drive. I rented books on self-help, philosophy, religion and business. This thing that many would have considered being a negative has afforded me such a great opportunity for growth that I would never have thought it possible. My horizons have been expanded greatly by looking for a positive opportunity in a negative situation.

I learned more driving back and forth to work listening to audio-tapes than I could have if I had attempted to sit and read these books. In the car there are no interruptions or distractions. I don't think about stopping to read or going for a walk or somebody walking in on me. I had a clear hour time slot twice a day that I allotted to my education. A huge obstacle I was able to overcome by wearing away at the issue but not fighting it head on. I became one with the problem and embraced it, thereby conquering it.

In adversity,
Remember to keep an even mind

—*Horace*

Happiness is not the absence of conflict,
But the ability to cope with it.

—*Anonymous*

Lesson 23

Water And Sales Mix Well

Many sales people are under the misconception that in order to be a successful salesperson you've got to close your client on the first try and move on to the next person. WRONG! Sales are built on the water principle, sales are built on relationships, building relationships takes time. For an example I can tell you that if somebody calls me today to take karate lessons, my first goal is not to get them into the door to sign up. Firstly, I want to educate them. I will ask many questions about their interests. I will invite them to come down to try a class and spend time watching them and talking to them. If, after the class, they are not sure if they would like to start training I invite them to come the next day for a second class. I ask them to come take the class so that they can give me their honest feedback about the instruction and style as well as the facility. Then after their second class I will sit with them and talk over what they thought. If I find out what I do is not for them, some people find this style of martial arts very demanding on the body and time committed, I can refer them to a school that might better suit them. In either case I keep in touch with them calling from time to time to see how they are making out.

I must add, most people who get past the first class will sign up because they see the benefit of how this school functions on the water principle. One of the senior students always works hand in hand with the new person and overcomes all of their objections before they arise. This gives the person a certain level of comfort that makes them want to stay. They are happy that after just one hour they have made a new friend and are already on the way to bettering themselves through a practice that will last a lifetime.

If however they don't sign up, I still treat them the same. When I call I talk to them about their training and life. Many people who didn't sign up at my school have been the source of referrals for me. They remember that I really do care. My goal wasn't to get them in the door, get the cash and go. I wanted to take their best interest and help them. People appreciate it when you are sincere. Long term relationships are the key to success.

I believe that unarmed truth and unconditional love will have the final word in reality.
This is why right, temporarily defeated, is stronger than evil triumphant.
—Martin Luther King Jr.

Lesson 24

Perseverance

One does not fail until he gives up

If you consider any obstacle you have as a journey then you understand that you have not failed as long as you are on the path. The only person who loses the race is the person who stops running. The winners in life are those who don't give up. Giving up is easy, but perseverance is for the truly brave.

There is a story about a man who was mining in Canada. For more than 10 years, while everybody else had given up, he continued his pursuit. He knew there would be a reward if he just dug a little deeper than the others. Most people had forgotten that he was still digging when in mid 1998 he came upon the largest diamond mine in North America. With this discovery, Canada will produce nearly 10% of the world's diamonds and the person who just wouldn't quit is a now millionaire.

How much deeper do you need to dig to get to the diamonds or to close that large sale or to land the account? The warrior knows that if he pushes just a little further when all others give up that he'll win.

If I am building a mountain
And stop before the last basketful of earth is placed on the summit,
I have failed.

—Confucius

Lesson 25

My First Sales Job

When I was 15 years old I wanted to get a job in sales. I had already been training in the martial arts for a few years now and needed some extra income. I drove my moped down to the local electronics store and asked for a job. I stood in the doorway and looked at the location and felt comfortable knowing that I would enjoy working there. I asked to see the manager and Jerry came out. He shook my hand and asked if he could help me. I said, "No, but I think I can help you. I'm looking for a job as a salesperson." He told me that he had enough sales people and I was too young. Using my newly gained warrior skills I persisted. I didn't believe that any place could have enough sales people as long as there was product on the floor to sell. I told him that I was eager to work and that I love electronic equipment. The answer was still no. I asked him what he had to lose. "I will work for you for one week, no questions asked. After that week you'll see if you can use my abilities." He was breaking down. I said, "To top it off, don't pay me, only give me a percentage of what I can sell for you." How could he say no at this point? He said ok.

I started that day. I asked him to show me all of the equipment and let me read the literature on it. I studied the equipment and took home flyers on the various products. The next day I showed up 15 minutes early and asked a few questions that had arisen out of my perusing the literature the night before. Astonished at my questions, Jerry asked if I had read all those flyers overnight, which of course I did. I was a warrior. Anything that I undertook I would do with 100% of my heart and soul. This is one of the first lessons that I learned through my martial arts training. If you intend on being really good at something, you must do it 100%.

Finally, my first chance. A very sweet middle aged lady walked in and handed me a needle for her phonograph. She was upset and told me this broke just before a party she had planned. All through her party she couldn't listen to her favorite records. I asked her how old the stereo system was and she told me she had received it as a gift 8 years ago. I continued to ask more and more questions to find out as much information as I could about her needs and current equipment. We had a wonderful conversation and built quite a rapport. I showed her how far stereo equipment had come in the last few years. I told her how amazing I found all the facts that I had read just the previous night and showed her the equipment of which I spoke. She was truly impressed. I told her that these new systems come with a warranty that is covered in the home, and that a problem like she had would have been solved before her important party. She played with all the dials and knobs. I put her favorite music on and told her to make herself comfortable while I researched how much this needle will cost her to replace. I went in the back and watched her from the office window. She was having a blast. I came back out a few minutes later with the information, actually two pieces of information. "Ma'am, the replacement needle for your system is $15.95, and you want to know something funny? For $30.00 down you could take home that great new system you have been enjoying." Well no sooner said than done the stereo was in the delivery truck on its way to her house. She called the manager to thank him for hiring a person who cared enough to look out for her best interest. I was immediately called into Jerry's office. "Do you know who I just got off the phone with Robert?" I did not. "Ms. Smith called and said she came in for a needle for her stereo system and left with a new stereo system." Now I remembered. "I see." Jerry pushed further. "I guess it is time to take you off of commission and hire you on full time." I asked if we could discuss this after my shift because I did not want to miss any potential sales. He agreed. Afterwards, we talked for about an hour. I did not want to give up on my ability to make commissions, so I asked to stay on the current salary structure I had. I stayed and worked with Jerry for the entire summer and worked part time after that for another 4 months.

Just an additional note, it is Jerry I have to thank for introducing me to the motivational power of Zig Ziglar. Jerry gave me several of Zig's tapes as bonuses for great sales. I have used much of the knowledge I have gained from the great Zig Ziglar my life. I would often compare his philosophy to that of the warrior strategists and they were very similar. Zig says, "You can get anything in life that you want if you just help enough other people get what they want." I carry this lesson in my mind and in my heart everyday and through every interaction.

Nothing in the world can take the place of persistence.
Talent will not: nothing is more common than unsuccessful individuals with talent.
Genius will not; un-rewarded genius is almost a proverb.
Education will not; the world is full of educated derelicts.
Persistence and determination alone are omni-important.
—Calvin Coolidge

Lesson 26

A Spark Lies Inside

Each person reading this book has within them a spark that can enable you to persevere in the face of obstacles. Obstacles that lie in our path are not meant to stop us, they are meant to help us along the way. If all of your goals could be attained without one single obstacle, you would not understand the true meaning of the goal. In sports, injuries are a huge obstacle. Many people who study martial arts set their goal on becoming black belts. In fact I have not met a person who is not, even if just slightly, enamored with the person who has earned a black belt. It is a great achievement. When I was a boy beginning my training it seemed like an out-of-this-world goal, with a million things in the way of its accomplishment. I welcomed anything that would stand in my way and set out not only to become a black belt, but to become a **seventh degree black belt**. It was a bizarre goal, because at that time I didn't even know a person ranked above second degree black belt. And to note, a person can only promote you to seventh degree black belt who is at least an eighth degree black belt. To me that was not an obstacle. I knew that at some point in my life I would meet a master who would promote me. Immediately important for me was to train, and train so hard that I would be ready when I met this ominous master. It is exactly what I did. For more than 3 years without any inkling that I might be making any headway in meeting the master, I knew that now I was in peak physical condition. I imagined the master in my mind testing me, training me and promoting me. I have to add that the number of the rank was not as important to me as the knowledge I had to possess to carry that rank. I studied, read, meditated and learned everything physical, spiritual and psychological about the martial arts, their history and styles. When I met the master that eventually promoted me the very first thing he said to me *was "There exists a spark in you that few people have; it is from that spark that a master will develop."*

Since then I have been fortunate enough to see how to pick up on that "spark" in others. It is quite interesting to watch people who possess this spark. They themselves often don't know that they possess it. Watching them grow and develop in any sport or career is exciting. Frustrating is when these people give up because they think they are failing due to a few obstacles that stood in their way. The only person who loses is the person who gives up. Everyone with drive and focus has the ability to become the manager, boss or CEO. The key to becoming a master of success is to overcome the small obstacles that stand in the way. If you beat an obstacle when it is small, it will never grow up to try and stop you.

> *If we are facing in the right direction,*
> *All we have to do is keep on walking.*
>
> *—Buddhist proverb*

Lesson 27

Journey vs. Destination

I remember teaching martial arts at the prestigious Sports Club/LA in the early nineties. I had several students that were coming along the ranks. Often I would talk to them about philosophy and history, I have always found it important to share with my students the spiritual energy that goes into the physical makeup of the art. One of my favorite lessons I have ever talked about was the *Journey vs. Destination*. I personally thought this would be far beyond the reach of most of my students. Surprisingly enough I was wrong. Several months after this lesson, the girl I was dating wrote it back to me. It meant so much to me knowing she had listened and heard what I had said and meant by this important lesson. I share it with you here.

I know there are times you feel very down and negative. *It is important however to remember that life is a journey. The destination is not as important as the people, places and things you touch along the way.* Life is a continuous journey. The destination should exist as a marker, as opposed to a goal. If your goal as a student of the martial arts is to attain the level of first degree black belt, one day you will get there, however your training will not be as complete as the student whose goal it is to be a good martial artist. Do not overlook the day to day beauty of things whether it be daily regimented training, exercise, diet, meditation, focus, struggles, battles, relationships, successes or failures. Each experience will strengthen you and will make you a better person. The seemingly arbitrary experiences you will encounter should be noted. The people you touch or that touch you have a specific meaning, don't overlook them. While on this journey, I remind you, to stay clear on your aspirations, your goals and your principles and morals. If while on this journey you are taken in different direction, be clear about what you are doing, but understand why you have now chosen a different path. In essence you are still on the journey you set out on; you just learned a valuable life lesson that has steered you a bit differently. Do not allow yourself to be swayed by the wicked paths of people, or by the easy way out. People can sometimes be evil and sway you from pure thoughts and pure actions. Remember, if the easy way is taken early on, it will increase the difficulty in the future. I focus on the joy I get from being on the journey of life. The beautiful plants I see on my way to a friend's house sometimes bring me more enjoyment than my actual destination. Have you ever taken the time to examine the sun rising or setting? Why doesn't it just come out and go down? There is so much drama and beauty that goes along with these seemingly simple things. Animals enjoy the sunrise and sunset. Dogs bark, birds sing. What do humans do? Here is one of the most miraculous things, and we overlook it. Strengthen your basics. All of the most complicated situations in life can be solved with the most basic of basics. Remember that my training took me from the basics to the intermediates, to the advanced, then to the most complex, in the end everything led back to the basics.

Simplicity is making the journey of this life with just enough baggage.
—Anonymous

Lesson 28

Learning Your ABC's

If you think it is hard to overcome obstacles, think of how hard it is to acquire the skills we need to learn to read and write. Fortunately, they are learned while we are still children. Think about the people that you've seen that are unable to connect the sounds and phonetics of letters and words. Then think about how hard it would be to teach that to somebody.

It all starts with the basics. First a child learns his or her ABC's. Then there are the simple words, then small sentences, and so on. Soon the child is able to read paragraphs and books. But remember it started with the ABC's. This is what you need to address to yourself.

Any obstacle that you face must be broken down into the ABC fundamentals. Take the book and break it into pages, break the pages into paragraphs, the paragraphs into sentences, the sentences into words and the words into letters. It is that simple with everything.

If you look at the complexity of a master guitarist, understand that he is just playing notes. Every person with two hands can put one finger on the fret-board of a guitar and pluck the string with the other hand. Then why can't everyone be a Paco Delucia? It takes rehearsing these basics repeatedly and then adding to them one step at a time. Running through the bars on the neck of the guitar, playing chopsticks, rehearsing the sales presentation, talking through the personal problems, disciplining the self to avoid fatty foods; every obstacle can be beaten if you learn your ABC's.

Take the time now and address what obstacles you need to overcome and break that obstacle into the ABC's. If it your goal to buy a house, you need to come up with a down payment. Perhaps you need $10,000.00. How will you earn that in your current job? Maybe you'll have to get a part-time job a few nights a week and save $500 a month. Let's say you and your partner did that. At the end of one year you would have the necessary $10,000. By curbing spending, you could save even more. Instead of going out on Friday night, how about a picnic Saturday afternoon? All the money you save can go into an interest bearing account and earn even more by years end.

> *Fear less, hope more;*
> *Eat less, chew more;*
> *Whine less, breathe more;*
> *Talk less, say more;*
> *Love more, and all good things will be yours.*
> *—Swedish proverb*

Lesson 29

No Means More

Many people interpret no to mean no. In most cases it means I don't understand. Even if the person you are dealing with is saying no to you at this point, chances are what they are refusing is the offer you proposed. In fact, I have never thought that anyone who said no to me was refusing me personally, they just didn't understand what I was proposing. Often upon re-proposing the offer, the person reconsidered.

Listen to where the objection comes in and use this to evaluate the reasoning behind it. The warrior looks at the adversary's attacks and uses them against him. This is the same principle that you must use in the marketplace. When the person says no, overcome the no, then move them toward your goal. If you just accept no as no, you will be shut down upon starting. Often the most joyous goals are met after overcoming a few objections. When the prospect says yes right away, you didn't sell him on the product, he had already made a decision before he met you. You, as the warrior, are there to convince and overcome. Use your tools to take away the ammunition one bullet at a time. Take the objections and answer the person's objections individually. Generally I will listen to two or three objections, then I will casually say, "Gee, you really are seriously interested in this. It's not often that someone comes up with such good questions about my service. What is it really that is keeping you from making your decision right now?" This will cut to the chase. When they disclose this point I reply, "Oh, I see. Is that the only thing holding you back?" To which they will generally answer *Yes.* "So if I can ease your concerns on this issue you're ready to get started today?" To which they again say *Yes.* Overcome this final objection and start writing the order.

It is important that you let the person voice their objections uninterrupted. Allow time between the person's objection and your reply. Many people don't understand the importance in this and they just jump right on the answer. I strongly disagree with this for a few reasons. *Firstly* the person should feel like you took the time to understand their question, that you sincerely care. Listening is a valuable tool that is hard to find. If you listen carefully to what people are saying, you appear to be more on their side than if you just slam an answer back at them. *Secondly,* it should appear that you don't hear these objections on a daily basis. If the answers are quick, the person will feel you are dealing with the objection not the person who gave you the objection. It should appear that you are happy they brought that up, because after hearing your answer to this one little issue, they will be much more able to make up their minds.

The obvious is that which is never seen
Until someone expresses it simply.

—*Kahlil Gibran*

Lesson 30

The Tentacle Principle

Whether it is a casual phone call to say hello or a note announcing what your business is doing, always have your tentacles out. Often someone will call me and just by speaking to them I will realize that there is something that they sell that I need. Getting an occasional note also makes you feel remembered.

An important thing to remember is that relationships are hard to start, but easy to nurture using the right tools. I have found that an occasional lunch with an acquaintance is a great way to catch up. I have a mailing list that announces almost anything I do in my field and I am always happy to add an acquaintance to it. If I see something that makes me think about someone in particular, I always call him or her to let them know that I thought of them or just drop them a short note.

A friend of mine Kevin Brewerton is a living example of this principle. I met Kevin two years ago through the martial arts. He was a European champion. More than being a champion in the martial arts he is also a champion in people skills. We had lunch a couple of times, worked out and hung out on a few occasions. Soon we became very good friends as a result of his skills. He would call at least once every other week to just say hello, see how things were going or see if time permitting we could grab a bite. I am not certain if he does this with everybody, but I know everybody likes him. I have yet to meet a person who has met this man who does not hold him in the highest regard.

Imagine the minimal effort that this concept takes. Put a few of the following principles to work for you as soon as possible. These strategies will wear away the borders and distances that exist between you and others.

Make at least 3 calls a day to people with whom you interact infrequently.

Write at least 2 thank you notes a week for leads, help, and advice or just for friendship.

Ask someone out to lunch at least once a week and discuss business, recreation or strategy (this is not a social lunch, discuss some business here).

When you find something that is of possible interest for someone you know, cut it out of the magazine, buy the book or drop them a line or a call and tell them about it.

Applying these principles will strengthen your ties to your allies and will keep you from slipping off the cliff. Any obstacle or objection that exists may only exist only due to unfamiliarity. Keeping relationships open and close keeps this from happening.

Each friend represents a world in us,
A world possibly not born until they arrive,
And it is only by this meeting that a new world is born.

—*Anais Nin*

Lesson 31

Winning At All Costs

My mom relates a funny story to me that explains why I am the way I am today. She would always tell my students, "There is nothing Robert hates more than losing." But while it is definitely true that I hate losing, one thing I hate more is someone else *letting* me win.

In losing we must consider ourselves winners. It is true that the lessons we learn through losing are those that give us the tools we need to acquire to win in the future.

Vince Lombardi said it best, "*Winning doesn't mean a lot, it means everything.*" I would like to add the following statement to this. *If by chance you happen to lose at something, make a winning experience out of it*. If you understand this, your losses will be few, because you will acquire the tools to win every time in the future.

The warrior uses his losses as opportunities. Look at the following examples.

** A mid level actor lost his contract from Warner Brothers only to end up President of the USA…. Who? Ronald Reagan.

** Henry Ford fired one of his workers who, in turn starting his own company… Who?

Lee Iococca

Good things happen to everyone. They lie just ahead if you keep your eyes open to the opportunity. There is always a reason when something ends, perhaps there was something wrong that you either knew about or didn't. Using these obstacles as stepping stones to move on and move forward makes you a warrior.

In order to master success you must accept the fact that there will be setbacks from time to time. How you deal with your setbacks is how you will fare in the long run. If failure sets you back without gaining an experience, you have lost. Learn from setbacks and make them your strengths. Use these strengths in achieving new goals.

Know thine opportunity.

—*Pittacus*

Men do with opportunities as children do at the seashore:
They fill their little hands with sand,
And then let the grains fall through,
One by one, till all are gone.

—*T. Jones*

Lesson 32

Where Should Your Mind Be?

Focusing your energy on what is important should be your primary goal. A great example lies in the many stories about Albert Einstein. It was reported that Einstein couldn't remember his own phone number. Every time people would see old Albert he wore a black suit. Although many thought he had only one suit because he was cheap, on the contrary he had in his closet a line of black suits. Why? His mind was too busy to have to think about what suit to where. By having all the same, the decision was made easier.

Henry Ford was once in court under examination by someone trying to prove him a fool. The person shot question after question at the man, all which he couldn't answer. When asked why he couldn't answer these questions he replied, " My friend, even though I can't answer these questions for you, I have many people in my employ that I can call and get these answers from."

Put your mind on what is important. Don't clutter your mind with trivialities. Focus on the big picture. Get over the obstacle and use the lessons you learned to benefit yourself and others. You mind must always be focused on the heart of the matter, be it winning the battle, closing the sale or getting your team to the Superbowl.

Concentrate your energies, your thoughts and your capital...
The wise man puts all his eggs in one basket
And watches that basket.

—*Andrew Carnegie*

Lesson 33

Don't Let A Blister Become A Callus

In training in such sports as karate, gymnastics or weight lifting, practitioners will allow their blisters to turn into calluses. The reason they allow this to happen is that once the soft, tender skin of the blister forms a callus there is no more pain in that region. The callus is a tough layer covering the pain, sheltering it from your mind and the nerve endings.

In a similar vein, many people let emotional and psychological problems become mental blisters. By not addressing what is bothering or causing you harm it forms a callus in your mind. That is to say, the problem still exists, but the mind is building a wall that is a callus of sorts.

It is important to cut off the problem while it is still soft and pliable, while it is still fresh in your mind. This "blister" that is brewing is a sign of a problem, an irritation that is demanding attention. This sign is staring you in the face. It will be easier to do something now, before it is too late. If you allow the problem to fester, eventually the pain associated with it will diminish. The problem is that it only diminishes in your mind. Look down, the problem is still there. Your mind has formed a thick mental callus that will be nearly impenetrable.

The warrior must examine problems that are "blisters" before they become calluses. Although it is painful to pop the blister, more important is the point of looking at that which causes the pain and addressing it.

If you are a manager and know of the insubordination of an employee and you do nothing about it, it will be your own fault if your department or company crumbles. Dealing with a situation while it is still fresh in your mind is the best, not necessarily the easiest, way to handle it. The skillful warrior watches for slight eruptions of fire and extinguishes them before they have the opportunity to flare up.

> *He becometh poor that dealeth with a slack hand:*
> *But the hand of the diligent maketh rich.*
>
> *—Proverbs 10:4*

Lesson 34

On Cheating

To start with I must advise you that winning by cheating is losing in the purest sense. To understand the concept of winning, we must understand that to win we have to overcome an obstacle. If there is no obstacle we have overcome nothing. If the boxer steps into the ring and his opponent does not show up, he has not won the fight, he has won by default. If the other fighter takes a dive in the third round, there still is not a clear victory, the fighter must overcome an obstacle to truly understand the concept of winning.

Some people are so in need of winning that they will do so at any cost, even if it means cheating. These people will stoop lower than imaginable to win at any cost. But be reminded that winning at any costs should never include cheating, because this is not winning. You will know inside that you have failed even though others may think that you have won. You, above all, must be able to face yourself in the end.

Winning by cheating is the lowest form of losing imaginable because not only have you not won, but also you have not lost anything by the lesson of losing.

If I am in a competition or in a negotiation I will go to the end of the world to win. However it remains important to win by winning with honor. If another person is needlessly hurt by my victory then it was not a true victory. Winning to me is everyone coming out of the game with something. So many people are asking themselves how the person who lost the game is a winner, or how they received any benefit. Simple they have not won the prize, but they have won the lesson. The prize on their behalf is the ability to better understand their reason for losing. This will, if properly received, strengthen character and desire. The person who never won a championship will want that prize stronger than the person who has won it for the past 3 years will. It is important that the person competing (as opposed to the one defending) keep his head clear and his goals pure.

> *The moral sense, or conscience, is as much a part of man as his leg or his arm.*
>
> —*Thomas Jefferson*
>
> *I would rather be the man who bought the Brooklyn Bridge than the man who sold it.*
>
> —*Will Rogers*

Lesson 35

The True Bonus May Not Lie In The Paycheck

Numerous bonuses and many gifts from clients rewarded all the years I worked as a bodyguard. My clients were always aware that I did a good job for them. People I worked with were always impressed with the professionalism with which I handled all assignments as well as any conflicts. Only one thanked me. Why is that so important? Simple, I put my life on the line everyday. Although most people don't understand this and think to themselves that bodyguards are overpaid, I invite you think again. I used to give potential clients the following example:

Let's say you think your life is in danger and you talk with a personal security specialist. He tells you that he will charge you $1000.00 a day to protect you, you think to yourself that you would take that job for that kind of money, many would. If, however, you knew somebody was going to put a hit on you a particular day and you knew they were serious, and, you knew they would follow through at any cost, now, how much would I have to pay you for a days work. I'm sure $100,000 wouldn't be enough.

My point is simple, this person is laying his life on the line everyday for an insignificant dollar value, and the money means little. I would always interview my client's before I worked for them. No amount of money in the world could get me to work for someone I thought little of. I did it for the money, yes, but most of all I did it for principle.

Thank you and recognition in the line of notes, pats on the back, commendations, etc. go a long way. The greatest example in the world is that of soldiers. Soldiers will fight with their lives for a medal. The greatest honor to a soldier is to have a medal pinned on his chest. Warriors understand recognition and use it wisely. If an employee does a good job reward him. There are countless ways you can reward employees; *plaques, letters of commendation, a special lunch, recognition at a department meeting, promotions*, and the list could go on forever. Use the tools you have wisely.

I always make it a habit to reward people in public and discipline them in private. This is perhaps one of the most valuable lessons you may learn from this book. Underline it and remember it. It will do you absolutely no good to ridicule / discipline a person in front of his peers, it will make them rebel against you. On the same hand, it will do you very little good to reward someone alone. People like others to know about their achievements and don't want anyone to know about their failures. The warrior-leader understands this.

> *We are all motivated by a keen desire for praise,*
> *And the better a man is,*
> *The more he is inspired by glory.*
>
> —*Cicero*

Lesson 36

Giving In vs. Giving Up

A warrior's decision-making progress can appear confusing to the layman. I will take a moment here to try to explain it to you. A true warrior can make a decision in what appears to be an instant. But don't be confused, much has gone into that decision. Years of knowledge and careful study of the situation are behind any decision the warrior makes.

If you want to be a warrior, plan accordingly. Anything that you think you may consider having to do must be planned for. If you think that eventually you will be presented with the opportunity to be wealthy, start preparing yourself now. This way you will know how to act when the opportunity arrives. See yourself in any part that you might imagine. From the day I started studying the martial arts, I imagined myself to have my own martial art school. I acted like it in everything I did. I carried myself like a master, even before I ever achieved the title. When I received the title, some of my students found out and pulled me aside to ask, "Sensei, we thought you already were a master teacher?" To me this was a big compliment. I never make it a habit to tell people what my rank or position is. If people don't see it in you, then they won't believe it if you tell them.

In decision making, it is crucial that you prepare yourself for the outcome of what you are dealing with. If you are buying a new car or selling the biggest prospect of this year, prepare yourself for any adversity that could befall you. The preparation must be tireless. Look at situation that may seem illogical to you. The more you look at it, the more you study it, the better you understand it, and the better off you'll be.

The concept of giving up before giving in is an important one to grasp. First of all we have to re-define the concept of giving up to mean to walk away, not to surrender. If you are forced to make a decision that you are not ready to make, it might not be a bad idea to walk away temporarily and regroup. Even if the other person tells you there won't be a second opportunity as good as this one, know when to fold up. There will always be a second opportunity, even though the second opportunity might not initially appear as good, you are in a better position to understand and benefit from it. You will gain immeasurable results over a rash decision in the first scenario. Allow your conscience to guide you.

In forty hours I shall be in battle, with little information, and on the spur of the moment will have to make the most momentous decisions.
But I believe that one's spirit enlarges with responsibility and that, with G-d's help,
I shall make them, and make them right.
—General George S. Patton

Lesson 37

Luck Is Opportunity Well Planned

Take these words and write them down somewhere where you can see them everyday and then get to work. Everything that you might wish to happen to you will in fact one day happen to you, so be prepared. Write down exactly what it is you want so your goals are clear. Never be jealous or envious of others who are successful. If you think that this should be you, write *that* down. If possible go to work with this person, or just become his or her friend. Learn from them, examine what they do.

If your goal is to meet the person of you dreams, prepare yourself. Write down the characteristics of this person and keep them in a place where you can look at them often. If physical characteristics strike you, get photos that resemble him or her. Hobbies, religion, ethnicity, anything that constitutes the makeup of this person must be on paper for you to read, hear and see.

If your goal is a promotion at work, write that down. Print yourself a business card with your name and desired job title and carry it with you. Look at yourself in the mirror and introduce yourself by your new title. Find out who is in that position right now and look at what his or her responsibilities are. Examine their personalities and characteristics. *Make them yours.* Please look at this last sentence carefully. I did not say imitate them, *I said make these traits yours.* This means put them into your routines and give them your own flare. Learn how to take on the responsibilities that they have. If there is a skill they have that you do not posses, learn it. It is an education for you, because on day you will need it.

And on the day that the perfect mate walks up to you or the promotion opportunity presents itself, seize it from in front of you. You don't even have to wait for it to come to you. Reach out and grasp it. You've done the homework, the legwork and the mental and spiritual homework necessary. Many will think, "Yeah, he's lucky." You'll know better.

> *Chance never helps those who do not help themselves.*
>
> —*Sophocles*
>
> *I'm a great believer in luck,*
> *And I find the harder I work,*
> *The more I have of it.*
>
> —*Thomas Jefferson*

Lesson 38

Obstacles That Don't Appear As Obstacles Are Obstacles None The Less

My sensei/teacher told me a story about his first trip to Japan. Already having achieved the rank of black belt, he searched out a fine school where he could further his studies of karate. He came upon the school of Master Soken. He entered the school and watched a bit of the class. After class he talked to Soken and asked if he could join the school. In the older days it was not about just signing up, you had to ask permission. Master Soken asked him to return to the dojo the next day in uniform and he did. A clean white, crisp uniform and a neatly tied black belt outfitted the strong American. He sat among the ranks of the other black belts in the line, but was not asked to join in with the class. Near the end of the session Master Soken noticed a look of bewilderment on his face. He was told he could spar with the girl at the end of the line. The frail girl wearing the green belt rose up and bowed to the strong American. "Begin" was called and that was about it. After several kicks to the midsection, punches to the face as well as a leg-sweep, he picked himself up and made it back to line. Needless to say, he continued to train at the school and was comforted to know that this frail young girl was the niece of the Grand Master, and many of the other students went through this same initiation ritual.

The moral of this story is, you don't know what the obstacle in front of you is until you meet it head on. If you immediately dismiss it as useless or worthless, you lose. Take the time to examine deeply and learn from it. From disappointment comes enlightenment. Use your lessons as guides to propel you further.

> *Be not afraid of growing slowly,*
> *Be only afraid of standing still.*
>
> —*Chinese proverb*
>
> *Men stumble over pebbles,*
> *Not over mountains.*
>
> —*Peretz (Yiddish writer)*

Lesson 39

Make Your Own History

The next time you face an obstacle, pretend you're watching a movie. Fast forward to the end to see how it turns out. Think about it. Let's say your obstacle is pushing a little harder on the close of the sale than you might feel comfortable. What's the outcome? If you don't push, and the client says "No", well, I guess you know the outcome there. If you push, only one of two things can happen, either:

The same thing that happens when you don't push, that is he'll still say no.

He will see your perspective a bit better and go with your suggestion.

By looking at the future, you give yourself an edge over your present.

Those who are unaware of the mistakes of the past are condemned by them in the future. Look at the lessons you've learned and apply them to your current place. Oftentimes when you look at a situation that has passed, you can see that the outcome was rarely as bad as you may envision it turning out. The key to your success will be conviction in what you say and a limited fear of the adverse.

In order to overcome obstacles we need to begin at the ground level. There is a wonderful story about the legendary strong man Milo. Milo was known to be one of the strongest men of all times. He started out simply, however. When the village cow had its first calf, Milo would pick it up and carry it into town. He carried it into town every day. Years later when the calf became an ox, Milo still carried it into town on his back. People were awe-struck by this act, but were not willing to pay the price of the years of training that went into his development of strength. Most people want results today without having done anything to substantiate these results yesterday. Great results have an enormous amount of work behind them. Start on your work today. If you want to eventually have a 32-inch waist, put down the ice cream cone today. If you want to have a million dollars, start saving your quarters today. Look into the future for what you want, then do the work today to substantiate these goals.

Every day someone, somewhere in the world achieves something great, whether it is a physical accomplishment, a financial achievement or a goal completed. In fact I would venture to say that more than once every day someone becomes a millionaire, not through the lottery alone, but through hard work and dedication. This will one-day be you. It has to be. If you have the dedication and perseverance there is no option but to achieve your goals. The person who made it just before you is no different, he only didn't give up when those who went before him did. Once you give up you are certain not to achieve the goal. As long as you are on the road to achievement you will one day make it.

To feel that one has a place in life
Solves half the problem of contentment.
—*George E. Woodberry*
If one advances confidently in the direction of his dreams,
And endeavors to live the life which he has imagined,
He will meet with success unexpected in common hours.
—*Henry David Thoreau*

Lesson 40

Conquering the Competition: The Fire Principle

To conquer our opponents we must first understand them.
To walk a mile in the opponent's shoes allows you to assess
your opponent's strengths and weaknesses.
Once you know his weaknesses you can turn them into your strengths.
Once you possess these strengths you can use them to demolish the
opponent.

Lesson 41

The Enemy—The Self

Remember that before you ever look to beat the enemy in front of you, it is necessary to do battle with the enemy inside of you.

Martial artists spend years discovering their own personal enemies. These enemies lie deep inside of us and must be faced. You must first understand yourself fully in order to be able to beat someone else. The more fully you understand yourself, your weaknesses, and your limitations, the less likely the opponent will be to attack them. Whether or not you will do battle, have a clear understanding of who you are and what you stand for. Analyze and deal with your weaknesses, physical or emotional. If your weakness lies in someone insulting your heritage, if this outrages you, deal with it. If you are unable to deal with someone yelling at you, deal with it. If you are fearful of getting hit, deal with it. If your weakness lies in your inability to say no to a crying person, deal with it, or it will beat you. You must come from a neutral place at the time of any battle. You must be certain of your place both emotional and physical. To begin with an unbeatable mind puts you ahead of the opponent before the battle ever begins.

To come to a clear understanding of your weaknesses may take a lifetime, however it is a challenge that will get easier once you begin. It requires deep introspection and honesty. You may be able to put up a charade and fool many, but you will not be able to fool yourself. Lying to the world is possible, lying to yourself is impossible. Try not to sweep your weaknesses under the rug. Eventually someone will come along and find them and exploit them. Take the time now and make a list of them. Write each one down and then next to them write down what you will need to do to overcome them. Meditate on this, take at least 20 minutes and think carefully. Recall things people may have said to you in the past, things like:

If you were just more flexible to other people's opinions.

If you just wouldn't get upset so easily.

Why do you always have to be right?

Why don't you stand up for yourself?

If you just weren't so cheap with your money.

How come you can't care about other people's feelings?

The important thing to do is to screen out statements that came up in arguments and out of negativity. Focus instead on the ones that hold objective insights toward your positive development. In order to change for the better, we must first be able to see when someone is telling us something that is meant to benefit us. If you have a hard time coming up with a list, ask a friend. I will point out that this should be a good friend. Ask him or her if there were two or three things that you could change about yourself, what should they be? If they are good friends, they will answer honestly.

Knowing others is wisdom,
Knowing yourself is Enlightenment
—Lao Tsu

Lesson 42

Overcoming One of
My Own Weaknesses

When I was a young boy I had a very weak stomach. My mom had to take me to the hospital several times for ailments and injuries. Many of my injuries in karate were stomachaches from being hit and not being able to continue afterwards. For many years I would try to avoid getting hit in the stomach. But of course, as you might know, this plight proved futile. Eventually my friend Scott and I learned to understand that we must address our weaknesses. Daily, in the hot Florida sun on summer break, we would fight for hours at a time to overcome fatigue and fear. When we realized our physical limitations we dealt with them one at a time. Finally it came the time to deal with my stomach weakness. I did thousands of sit-ups, leg raises and other conditioning exercises. It consumed me to strengthen my stomach. I read Arnold Schwarzenegger books, I went to the gym until eventually I beat the weakness. Arnold put it well in one of his books. He said that he looks at himself as a sculptor, examining each part of the body. Clearly seeing where more "clay" needs to be added and where some needs to be stripped away. I adopted this principle in so many aspects of my training. Once my stomach was conditioned I still had to face the fear of getting hit in the stomach. Daily we would stand in a corner and have our partner punch our stomachs. Getting hit over and over in the stomach accustomed me as to know how to tense up the stomach on impact. The ability to maintain a tight/strong stomach also proved beneficial. For years I would train my stomach even while driving in my car by just contracting the muscles continuously. It was a weakness that eventually became my strength.

Examine your own weakness and try to see how you can turn it into your strength. Don't give up on the first hint of failure. Each time you overcome a failure, you are conquering the opponent. To be a master of yourself you need honest self-evaluation followed by a fire/drive to deal with those limitations. Recognize that a chain is no stronger than it's weakest link, and, as if your life depended on it, strengthen that link.

What are your weaknesses? Are you afraid of standing in front of a crowd and presenting your product? Are you afraid to make a presentation to an executive? Do you feel more comfortable presenting to men or women? Do you not like to make sales calls on the phone? Whatever your weakness is, it will come back to haunt you eventually. Address the weakness now and you'll overcome it in no time.

Practice doing that what makes you feel uncomfortable.

Many sales people don't like to do a sales presentation when the decision-maker is not in the room. I love to. Why you ask? Simple. *First off*, it is a great practice-run. *Two*, the people listening, since they don't really have the power to make a yes or no decision are not going to be as critical of you as the big guy. *Three*, if I can get these people genuinely excited about my service or product, chances are they will sell it to the big guy, I won't have to. These people become my allies. Everything I do and say is geared toward them. I ask them questions. These people will not have a reason to put up their guards. They are my ace in the hole to find out anything and everything I want to know about my prospect. By presenting to these people, I am more than just presenting a sales-pitch. I am learning everything I need to know about my prospect.

The life which is unexamined is not worth living

—Plato

Lesson 43

Dazzle and Overwhelm

The energy of Conquering lies in the fire principle. Fighting and aggression is fire. Confrontation is fire, this is a very yang energy and must be used carefully. There are rare occasions in which we use the fire principle. But I must say, choose them carefully. The use of yang energy depletes you very quickly. The wise warrior chooses his battles carefully. Make certain that the battle you are going into is worth your while. Examine the situation carefully.

When you conquer a situation or opponent using the fire principle, you will dazzle and overwhelm them. You will not let up until the situation is totally conquered. Your opponent will be confused and overwhelmed, he will not know what hit him. This is the underlying principle of the fire strategy.

When I first started studying martial arts I was taught a principle that I carried throughout my personal and business life in one way or another. Never fight unless your life or honor is at stake. Fighting to me always meant any confrontation, not only physical, but also verbal. I am not one to run from confrontation if it is worthwhile. In fact I am the first to engage if someone weaker than me is in danger, if my honor is threatened or such. However, I am careful to assess the situation carefully and to be 100% certain about this. Energy wasted on a foolish battle is forever gone and can never be regained. The words that pass your lips are forever gone as well. They can't be reclaimed. Have you ever said something to someone and then wish you had never said that? Take that as a valuable lesson. Whatever that was it was a lesson for you.

Those who do not learn from the past are condemned by its mistakes forever.

If you are cornered and are required to use the tools of winning from an assertive place, I want them to be in your arsenal. There are however repercussions that you need to consider if you abuse these principles. The biggest is that they will one day be used against you. If you use them in the name of valor, of helping others you will be forever rewarded. Therefore use them to turn away situations that are evil and bad. My sensei told me once, "You never know who you're doing battle with, so choose your battles carefully," I give you the same advice.

Sometimes in using an aggressive nature you will find yourself in a down place, a place that you need to come out of quickly. You may feel bad and may even wonder why you are going to this place. The only advice I can give you is that you are here for either of two reasons, One, nothing else worked.

> Two, the opponent forced you there.
> You can't hold a man down
> Without staying down with him.
> —*Booker T. Washington*
> All foes are mortal
> —*Paul Valery*

Lesson 44

Fire in Confrontation
A verbal confrontation:

When this type of confrontation arises and you are threatened or someone/something you care about is threatened, come from a place of strength and strike immediately.

In the warrior days samurai had to make decisions of life and death before a sword was drawn. Those who waited until the last moment would perish. A warrior makes up his mind quickly, but is slow to change it. In times of conflict, sometimes it is necessary to annihilate and overwhelm your opponent. Don't let him see you think. Strike immediately.

I once remember seeing a person hitting a child in a department store. This is something I don't agree with even though I believe in discipline. A strong man hitting a small child is merely someone acting out of anger and not power. I immediately "crashed" his party and said to him some words that were less than kind. I knew that an insult relating to his mother and his size would certainly shift his focus over to me. I continued the barrage, not allowing him a place to enter. Mine was a fire principle. There was no room for argument, discussion or negotiation. He didn't know what hit him. I simply stated my point of view so intensely and powerfully he didn't have a chance to enter or counter. I continued my barrage of verbal attacks at him. I explained to him that what he was doing to his son could also happen to him. Someone could come out of nowhere and do these types of things to him and he would have no chance. He was dazzled and overwhelmed. He was at a total loss for words when I was through, even though he attempted to interrupt on several occasions. I knew I had him beat when he tried to speak but immediately fell prey to my words. After I finished my point, I simply turned and walked away. I have seen this type of assault used by cross-examining attorneys. They will simply ask a series of questions, then hammer the person with facts they had previously stated. Then they will finish by saying, "I have nothing further."

A more physical example:

I was working security at a party in a hotel in Hollywood. I got a call with a friend of mine that there was a guy trying to break into a room with a knife. We looked throughout the perimeter and found nothing, we separated and I found an individual with a knife. He was not a patron of the establishment. He immediately ditched the knife. I asked him if I could talk to him. He ran. I cornered him and tried to talk to him. I thought in my heart that maybe he had a reason for his actions. He told me to *buzz off* (not quite that nicely). I asked him to come downstairs with me, he refused. Another person arrived on the scene and disturbed the situation. The individual in question hit me with a right hook to my left eye. I thought ok, now that he's gotten that out of his system we could talk. But no, he was aiming for another one. Well, needless to say, here is where the fire principle came into play. Sometimes when a person acts out of aggression, they just need to get some steam off. If they need to yell at me to displace some aggression that they may have had with a co-worker or spouse that's ok. I'll listen and then talk to them. However, there are those times when someone is just too hostile, as was the case with my hotel situation. Once I noticed this, I assaulted with the fire principle. Within a few short moments he found himself handcuffed, in a squad car on the way to jail. The attacks I launched at him were meant to totally overwhelm him and not allow him even the slightest place for escape. Several weeks later I was informed that this person wanted to sue me for assault. I went to the court and saw him sitting there across from me, obviously having forgotten what had happened just a few short weeks ago. Here was a person who was so in the wrong and now he decides to make one wrong into two wrongs. I asked the lawyer who was assigned to represent me how someone could be so stupid. He told me to keep cool and he would take care of the whole thing. I thought that was the right answer for him to say since he, after all was getting paid by the hour. My mission was more important; I truly wanted to help this young man understand what had happened. Coincidentally he got up and left the courtroom, I excused myself and followed him quietly into the bathroom. We had a lovely chat (water principle), I reminded him that he was in the wrong, happily he saw my point of view. He then saw the benefit in dropping all charges. Upon returning back to the courtroom, he whispered something to his attorney. Our case was called before the judge. His lawyer stood up and said we would like to drop all charges filed. Wow, what a happy moment, a moment of victory.

I am not a big advocate of violence. In fact I have been successful enough in my life to avoid it most of the time. As a warrior I do however understand that sometimes we are forced to do that which makes us feel uncomfortable. If I need to go to a violent place I must not be afraid.

Become so wrapped up in something
That you forget to be afraid.
                                        —*Lady Bird Johnson*
...one may smile, and smile, and smile,
              and be a villain.
                                        —*William Shakespeare*

Lesson 45

Don't Give In

Sometimes in a negotiation or other situation you will need to employ the principles of the fire book. I must tell you that if you choose this way it is very strong. You can not let up on your assault. You can not listen to the other person's point of view. This is a very last resort method. You've already found the killer; he's standing in front of you with the smoking gun, now he's pointing it at you. *Fire principle time.* When I use this way, I use Musashi's principle of *forestalling him by attacking.* I do not give the opponent any opportunity to attack first. You must however remain calm. Never attack from a hostile place. Your thought must be collected and sane. If you find yourself in a rage, it is not the right time to attack. Retreat… It is the master warrior who can attack with the fire principle while remaining calm. When you use this, you will dazzle and overwhelm your opponent.

I once explained this principle to one of my clients that is a top entertainment attorney. I told him the fire principle comes into play when you've listened to the other sides total arguments. You've listened to all the evidence and are clear that the evidence you have shows he's incriminating himself. You now stand before him and cite everything that he's said, cite all the incriminating facts, cite the discrepancies, the inconsistencies and so forth. You don't stop for a pause; you assault like a tank, bang-bang-bang. Until there is nothing left to be said. Then you walk away. There is nothing left to be said by you, and in this case there is nothing further you need to hear. You state your case, overwhelm him, and leave nothing left to be said and leave.

We succeed only as we identify in life, or in war, or in anything else,
A single overriding objective,
And make all other considerations bend to that one objective.
                    —Dwight D. Eisenhower

Lesson 46

Counter on the Attack

The principle of fire is also used in fighting as follows. When a person attacks you he has a certain amount of momentum. This can ether be used against him or ignored. In martial art styles such as Tori-te and Ju-jitsu the opponents' strength is used against him. For example, if someone throws a punch at me and I can block that punch in time while he is still in motion from that strike and counterstrike him, I will benefit from his power. The result is as if a car was slamming head on into another moving car as opposed to a brick wall. In strategy you will use his point against him. You will attack his weakest point.

It is important to always remember to attack the enemies' weakest points. Look for them, aim for them, and reach them. If he makes two good points and one weak one, it is the weak on you go after. This takes careful planning and strategy. Your eyes must be open for the opportunity and your mind must be prepared with the ability to strike. If you allow the opportunity to pass, it may not come again, and thereby you will have lost your chance. It is always better to win at this principle by using the opponents' words or attacks against him. It proves strength and ability. You are allowing him the opportunity to strike first so to speak. You are coming from a high place. This also makes it really important to be a perceptive warrior. You must listen and observe at all times for the opportunity that surrounds you.

I remember once negotiating on a lease. The rate the landlord was asking was very fair, but too high for me to pay. I listened to their points. One, the property was worth more than I wanted to pay. Two, they already had someone else who would pay them what they were asking. Three, Every other tenant was paying higher rent. I negotiated on the first two, I knew that three I could not win on. I agreed that the property was worth more than I was able to pay. I used the word able, not willing. I combined the first and the second I expressed what I would do with the building, that I would build a business that the neighboring merchants would be happy to associate with. I would consult with them and help them in any fashion I could with regards to my specialty, martial arts. And when the business prospered I would offer them a fair additional percentage of revenues for rent. Needless to say, they agreed. Even though much of this situation seemed flexible and water like, I put myself in a fire/assertive place. I needed to win, I saw no other way out. In this strategy, as in all others, you must think of yourself as being in your enemy's place. If you understand this principle you will understand true strategy. It is explained well in the verse by Musashi, *"He who is shut inside is a pheasant. He who enters to arrest is a hawk."* The burglar in the house is surprised when the residents come home early, therefore, it is the burglar who is at a disadvantage. He is unfamiliar with the surroundings, the terrain and the people coming in. He doesn't know if they are armed, if there is one or a hundred. In taking advantage of this principle that gives us strength.

In a negotiation you must place yourself in control. Whether you want to get the sale, win the argument or win the fight you must understand the principle of using your enemy's weaknesses against him.

Great works are performed not by strength
But by perseverance.

—*Samuel Johnson*

Lesson 47

The Power of the Nod: Fire and Water Principles

I have interacted with many traditional Japanese people and learned an immense amount about them and their culture as well as what made their principles and philosophies so successful. If you ever watch the interaction between two Japanese people it goes as follows: One person talks, and the other person nods. He will continuously interrupt the person speaking with "Hai", translated means "OK". Over and over as the person speaking drones on, the listener will nod, nod, nod and repeat ok, ok, ok. To the outside we think everything is in agreement. Not so, what the listener is saying is that "Ok, I hear you." He would say so no matter what the context of the conversation was. It is a polite way to keep the interaction between the two going.

It is a very polite way of keeping the conversation moving. Generally the listener will not interject his opinion until it is his turn. At that point the roles shift. It is now the other person's turn to nod and say OK. At that point the speaker will focus on his points that might be slightly different and place focus on them. Eventually the two have bantered back and forth enough to come to an amicable conclusion.

Conversely, in Japan, it is generally considered rude to just sit and listen to the person talking without interruption. You appear to the other person not to be interested in what they are saying. By letting the person talk and talk, you allow him to further open himself up. If there are any weaknesses, you allow and encourage them to be seen by moving the conversation forward.

If you consider the person you are dealing with as an enemy and you don't yet know enough about him, this little principle will work wonders in allowing you to learn more.

> *No matter what accomplishments you make,*
> *Somebody helps you.*
>
> —*Althea Gibson Darben*

Lesson 48

A Peaceful Principle of Conquering

The Japanese have a wonderful term, Mu Te Katsu Ryu (system of victory without fighting). This is an ideal way of facing almost any confrontation. Here you will surround a situation and place it under control. The situation cannot be forced under control; it must be brought there by careful techniques. To force it there is impossible; to force anything is impossible. Anything that is forced ultimately breaks: it is not my goal to break anything, only to accept and fix. Many people studying the martial arts occupy their minds with fighting their enemy; this is the wrong concept. Once you accept the fact that there is an enemy you are already defeated. When I step on the mat, whether it is at the dojo or on the mat of life, I deal with only one thing, myself. The person in front of me is merely my canvas; his ukemi (fall) will reflect my technique as the canvas interprets the artist's brush stroke. It does not influence it or change it. How could it?

If it is my idea to irimi, or enter, then I will do that no matter what his technique. If you consider this person an opponent you are fighting him in numerous battles, you must make this man your partner. The lion-tamer and the lion seem as opponents on the outside, but who in their right mind would enter a ring with an opponent against whom they knew they had no chance? These partnerships are carefully planned and developed. This planning in Budo may take years i.e. teacher/student, months student/student, or a fraction of a second attacker/defender. To overcome our opponents through violence is not only stupid, it is impossible. A firefighter understands this concept. Water, the opposite element of fire is used to fight the fire. Therefore it is no longer a fight. The water will overcome the fire; it will encompass the flames and therefore will end the destruction. Water, an element I will tell you much about later is nature's answer to fire. To fight is a needless concept. Embrace and make peace. What good ever came from war? Needless lives are lost before the leaders of both sides sit down at a table to make peace. The respective leaders are never injured. In fact, it is against international law to assassinate the head of a country / nation. It is against the law of G-d and man to murder. However, when a country calls a war, this country not only turns its back on these laws, but it advocates their breakage. Why? Because the other country is considered to be the enemy. Why is it considered the enemy? Because the leader of the country said so. If you object to this you are jailed. You become stripped of your rights because you thought on your own accord. To make a war that will end in a peaceful negotiation is wrong, dead wrong. Please, I appeal to you, use your head, if it is your ultimate goal to sit down and hammer things out across a table, then begin by doing this. We must spare the innocent lives.

It is forbidden to kill, therefore all murderers are punished unless they kill in large number and to the sound of trumpets. —Voltaire

The philosophy of conquering remains in the fire element. The reason for this is because the fire element implies an overwhelming consummation of the situation at hand. Fire, more than most elements encompasses and smothers. If it is your goal to conquer, you will be using a basic fire principle. How you will apply the principle will be up to you.

The peaceful warrior will choose a path of amicable resolution. However it is his all-consuming principle to be peaceful and conquer in that way. The rogue warrior will choose to overwhelm and startle his opponent and win in this fashion. In either case both warriors have used a fire principle of sorts. To conquer requires the use of fire principle. It must be your all-encompassing thought to conquer. You don't have to convince the person 100% to your point of view, if this is not your goal, but you must come to a resolution.

Lesson 49

Practice Just Isn't Enough

The misconception that practice makes perfect is the first thing you should strike from your mind if you want to succeed. Practice does not make perfect, perfect practice makes perfect. Just repeating something will instill the movements into your subconscious mind and will even begin to train muscle memory, but if incorrectly learned these movements will take countless years to overcome. Anyone who does not understand this is certain to fail in his or her own tracks. So often a person begins an activity such as karate and feels that by showing up they will succeed. Although this may be the case with some instructors, traditional instructors will physically throw you out of the dojo for wasting their time.

Often I would teach a class in which students did a thousand kicks in one class, a good self-discipline and a great workout. Younger, more flexible students often show off their kicks with how high they can kick. Over and over they kick to the level of their own chests. The problem is that a front kick is not effective to that region because that is where the opponent's arms will be and they will therefore be able to protect him. The front kick is meant to be landed in the lower region, between the groin and the bladder. The student who constantly practices his kicks high and then thinks that he will simply shift them lower when a true confrontation comes is in for a surprise.

What you have been rehearsing for all of your years of practice is what will come out in a fight. If you've trained 3 years, 3 times a week, 2 hours a day to kick high and suddenly, under an immense amount of pressure such as a fight, you think you'll be able to re-think your strategy, you're in for a surprise. You won't even have time to think.

Therefore, perfect practice makes perfect. Understand 100% what you are doing and why. Spend the time dissecting the technique, the sales call, the product you sell, the objection that you need to overcome and train for that. Your technique must be 100% in practice as it will be in application. You are leading yourself down a false road thinking you will make it up as you go along.

The businessperson can learn a lot from the fighter. The fighter moves carefully in for the kill, as the salesperson or manager should move in for the objective that he seeks. The fighter has a carefully rehearsed and planned strategy to follow in order to obtain his objective. Yet he remains empty of ego or judgement. The manager or salesperson should also have a carefully rehearsed and planned strategy. The fighter will continue to assault until the opening he is looking for is available and then he will strike, as should the businessperson. There are numerous ways to look for the opening and create it, the master looks for and finds the way. The master is prepared for the obstacle before it arises and when it does he can easily and quickly shift his techniques without any conflict.

The greatest obstacle to discovery is not ignorance,
It is the illusion of knowledge.
—Daniel J. Boorstin

Lesson 50

Know Your Opponent Better than Yourself

He who knows not, and knows not that he knows not,
Is a fool; shun him.
He who knows not, and knows that he knows not,
Is a student; teach him.
He who knows,
And knows not that he knows, is asleep; wake him.
He who knows, and knows that he knows,
Is wise; follow him.

—Asian proverb

In many of the chapters of this book I talk about knowing yourself well. It is also very important to know your opponent. In fact it should be your goal to know your opponent better than yourself. Know his hotspots, his buttons, his likes or dislikes. In saying *the opponent* it is important to understand that I mean the person with which you are dealing, not necessarily an adversary.

When I present a proposal to someone I outline what I am prepared to say and also any objection that I know could possibly be brought up. Many people wonder how I could know what objections the other side could bring up, simple, I put myself in their shoes before I present the proposal to them. I sit in an imaginary chair and listen to my proposal and then write down my own objection. That's right, my own objections to my own proposal. I work these objections back into my proposal, and continue to polish the proposal until it works.

Some simple objections are always used. For example, managers are always bringing up the fact that you don't have enough experience. Which leads me to add the following into almost all presentations when necessary: *"I know there are a lot of people with more experience who could fulfill this position. But I bring to the table a fresh outlook and an energy that will outshine the old **what needs to be done in this position**".* Generally, people like fresh energies and the **whatever it takes mentality**. If you have this, not much will get in your way.

This concept can be used in personal relationships, sales and business meetings. You simply need to put yourself into the other person's shoes and see things from their point of view. Keep an open mind and take notes. Be objective and learn from your mistakes. If you come across one you've never heard, objections that is, say so. "Wow, you know nobody has ever brought that up before. In fact in the 3 years I've been working with this company I thought I understood any and all concerns someone might have, but I certainly appreciate this opportunity to address this." Address this then continue on with your presentation. Honesty is often the best answer. If you don't know something, make it your point to find out. Go to the end of the world to find out, your life will become a mission.

You only need to find out something once, then you know.
But you can not know something for the rest of your life.

Lesson 51

Allowing the Competition to Conquer Themselves

Allow the fire that burns too brightly to burn itself out, without you getting burned.

In my career as a businessperson and bodyguard, I often was confronted by verbal assaults. On any one of these occasions I could easily have launched counter attacks and won the battle with ease. However, I learned a powerful tool to overcoming someone who is in a rage: You allow the person to exhaust his or her anger. Just as the fireman often must wait while the inferno to burn itself out, so must you be able and willing to do the same. The person assaulting you verbally will burn himself out at some point. The important factor for you is to add nothing to the assault, therefore just pull back. I would often allow the person to attack, insult, rage and whatever as they wished. In fact the louder they got the quieter I got. This tends to infuriate the attacker more than anything else does. In fact it ignites their fire so strong inside of them that it eventually burns itself out. This is my goal in this situation. My comment back to people in this type of rage was generally just repeating their statements back to them in the form of a question. Sooner or later the person will come back to their senses. When they are starting to run out of things to shout about, a good tactic to drain the assault is to ask, very nicely, *"Are you finished?"* If they are, then I go to leave and ask them if we can talk again in 24 hours. Giving them this opportunity will usually end with an apology from them later. If you are big enough to let them get *it* out of their system, the frustration will burn itself out. Sometimes when somebody starts to complain about something, even if it is me, I will add to their complaints. Example: *"Yes, but you know the worse part of what I did was _____."* This lets them see that you are just human, and accepting of your wrongs.

Remember, anything that burns too brightly will eventually burn itself out. It's the simmering fires that burn much longer and more dangerously than the infernos.

The lesson to be learned here is that if you encounter someone on a rage, your best tool may be to do nothing. Allow them to burn themselves out instead of jumping in and getting burned.

When people are least sure,
They are often most dogmatic.
—John Kenneth Galbraith

Lesson 52

Never Let 'em Know When You're out of Ammo

There is an old example of this in which Clint Eastwood as Dirty Harry is involved in a shootout and fires off several rounds from his 44 Magnum *"the world's most powerful handgun"*. He rushes up to the criminal and points it at his head and says, *"You know in all this confusion I'm not sure if I fired off 6 shots or 5, so you have to ask yourself if you feel lucky. Well, do ya, punk?"* You know the rest. It is a classic line in strategy. If the other side is not sure if you're out of ammo or still fully stocked they will naturally assume your still stocked, especially if you lead them to think that.

This principle is useful in martial arts as well as business. If you're involved in a negotiation, never let 'em see you sweat. Even if all the chips are down and failure is right in front of you, stand up tall and keep smiling. If you don't know what to say, say nothing at all. Stay composed. This is the most important part. Self-composure is paramount in negotiations. Self assurance and conviction can make anyone change their point of view, even if they thought they were right in the first place. You just need to figure out who has a stronger conviction, you or them. It's the old poker face principal. If you've ever played cards with someone who bluffs well you'll know what I'm talking about.

Many years ago I was in Washington DC and met this guy who was a chess champion. He truly was one of the better players around, but also had a big head as a result of it. He would constantly boast of his accomplishments and would challenge anyone to play for any sum of money. I asked him how he would feel about a challenge. He agreed. I told him that I was also a champion and had only been defeated once, by Bobby Fischer. He couldn't believe it. This was a man who was so full of himself, yet I chose to challenge him merely for the fun of it. I asked him how he felt about the sum of $2000.00. He looked at me carefully and thought it over. He said, "Hey, why don't we just play for the fun of it." I agreed. We sat down, many people watched. We tossed a coin for first move, and he won. He moved a pawn; I followed with a pawn as well. After several movements he became aware of the situation, *I had no idea how to play chess.* He was duped. I called his bluff and he lost. He could have played me for two grand and won. He was a champion, yet a person who doesn't even know the basic movements of the pieces had fooled him. How frustrating for him. I always love to play jokes on people, but I tell this story to you here for an important reason, learn how and when to bluff. But what will serve you even better is never get too big of an ego to let it get the best of you.

A man's doubts and fears are his worst enemies.
—*William Wrigley Jr.*
Confidence imparts a wonderful inspiration to its possessor.
—*John Milton*

Lesson 53

Don't Underestimate Yourself, While You Overestimate the Competition

The warrior, although remaining humble, always keeps himself ahead of the competition. It is important to do this in a humble way. Not to be conceited or rude, we need to feel confident about ourselves and our ability to outperform others. Whether it is being able to get the account or land the job we're applying for, always rank yourself ahead of the competition.

On numerous occasions I have applied for jobs that by most respects I was considered under-qualified for. Under-qualified in most people's eyes, but not in mine. I always approached the situation with what I could bring to the table. If my experience didn't measure up to the others, I explained how a fresh outlook could change the entire perspective of the company or product for which I would be working. If I was too young, I explained the enthusiasm and energy I would bring with me. Too old, I spoke of the experience and knowledge I possessed, etc, etc. You get the idea. I never let a lack of something from the outside be a lack in my ability to get where I wanted to go.

It has always been my opinion that if someone else can do it, so can I. Remember at some point someone started with nothing more than determination and trial and error. If you possess the same thing, you possess the tools of the great minds of all time. You will challenge the establishment, the nay Sayers and the critics. Believe in yourself and go.

The confidence which we have in ourselves
Gives birth to much of that which we have in others.
—Francois de La Rochefoucauld

As soon as you trust yourself,
You will know how to live.
—Johann von Goethe

Lesson 54

All the Training in the World Can't Change This...

Enthusiasm outweighs experience 100 to 1. There are hundreds of people in training everyday learning job skills that will allow them to perform within their specific duties. You can learn to type, to repair, to clean, to build, design, and so on. However, you can't learn enthusiasm. That is why it outweighs every other skill. It is in fact not a skill; it is a characteristic, a characteristic of a motivated person.

> *A man can be short and dumpy and getting bald*
> *But if he has fire,*
> *Women will like him*
> *—Mae West*

Enthusiasm is contagious. If you've ever been in the room with someone who is a ball of energy you'll notice one of two things:

You too will become energetic and motivated.

You will suddenly feel tired and irritated.

If (b) is the case, there is good reason to examine yourself. Chances are you are a person that is *keyed* very low, you are lacking inspiration.

A person who lacks inspiration cannot handle surrounding themselves with enthusiastic people. In fact they stick out like a sore thumb. It's almost like a sinner in a room full of saints. The person feels awkward and out of place. Examine yourself next time you are surrounded by motivated people. In the same respect examine others in the room if you are the person doing the motivating. Change your perspective and your outlook and everything will soon be brighter.

There once was a monk who lived in a hut on top of a mountain. He had no possessions and lived a simple life. One night he went down to the village. Upon returning to his hut he noticed a burglar inside. The burglar was stunned to find nothing inside the hut; there was nothing for him to steal. The monk feeling sad said to the burglar, "You poor man, you have made this journey yet I have nothing for you to take." At which point he removed his own clothes and gave them to the burglar. The burglar was bewildered and left. The monk sat naked under the moonlit sky and said to himself, "I only wish I could have given him this beautiful moon."

You see the monk's perspective was that even though all his possessions were gone, he was still in possession of the greatest of all possessions, the gifts that no one can take. How often are we not grateful for the simplest pleasures? The food we eat, our clothes, family and friends, a warm bed to sleep in. etc., etc. The more grateful we are, the more we can achieve. Be enthusiastic about what you have, who you are and what you want.

> *If you aren't fired with enthusiasm,*
> *You'll be fired with enthusiasm.*
>
> —*Vince Lombardi*
>
> *A man can succeed at almost anything*
> *For which he has unlimited enthusiasm.*
>
> —*Charles Schwab*

Lesson 55

You Can't Do That

Warriors don't listen to can't. In fact they can't listen to can't. A great story that relates this is a young man who lived in Texas who wanted to make a film. He had never made a film before and had never gone to film school. He knew nothing about making a film except that you put film in the camera, put people in front of the camera and roll. He didn't know about the rules, the technical things that could hinder production, or any other things that would stand in the way of shooting a movie. He got together enough money to buy the film and a few other incidentals. How he got the money together is another story, for that read his book "Rebel Without a Crew" by Robert Rodriguez. He shot his first movie for $7000, something that anyone who knows anything would tell you is impossible.

Anyone who knows anything may know *less* than someone who knows *nothing*.

Education can sometimes be a hindrance. If you look at all the probabilities that have come through standardized education you may understand what I'm trying to say. Man can't fly. Man can't go to the moon. Computers, atoms, artificial limbs, the four-minute mile, the light bulb, etc., conventional people who never **learned** to *know better* have often shattered conventional thinking. If you use education, use it to look at what "can't" be done, and then set your goals on achieving these.

> *What we learn to do,*
> *We learn by doing.*
>
> *—Aristotle*
>
> *Wisdom is not wisdom*
> *When it is learned from books alone.*
>
> *—Horace*

Lesson 56

A Lesson on Competition

Sitting on the mat as a young warrior I saw an ominous man pacing in front of me. He told the class many stories about history, exercise, war and martial arts. One of the things I remember most vividly is his account on how many of us would fail. In his own words:

"I'd like you to look next to you, look to your left and to your right. By the time you reach brown belt, one of those people won't be sitting there any more. Now, look a bit further up and down the mat, by the time you reach black belt, better than 75% of the people now on the mat won't be there any more. And if you dare, look at the mat as a whole. If you achieve the rank of master, chances are you will be the only person in this group to survive."

I knew this applied to me. I looked up and down the mat and noticed all of their faces. Most appeared with an "I don't care attitude", not me, I challenged this notion. A bit more than 20 years later I have achieved the rank of master teacher, and the truth be known, not one of these people that I started with is still active in the practice of the martial arts.

Look at this as a goal in your job. If you want to move up the ladder of success, you will pass many people on the way. Keep in mind that they too may have the same outlook. You will have to out-maneuver them. Think into the future; think like you are already the manager, CEO, Vice President, or whatever your goal may be. From the first day I practiced martial arts, I practiced as though I was a master. I wasn't sure what a master would practice like, but I made it up in my head. I saw myself as the master, and today, that is where I am. If I can do it, you can to. All the tools I used to achieve these things are written in the pages of this book, read them carefully, highlight the ones that mean a lot to you. Use this, and all books, as a guide to self-help, not idle tools for recreation. Write down the things that could change your life and carry them around in your wallet. Positive thinking leads to positive results.

> *All that we are is the result of what we have thought.*
> *The mind is everything.*
> *What we think, we become.*
> —*Buddha*
> *Optimism and humor are the glue of life.*
> *Without both of them we would*
> *Never have survived our captivity.*
> —*Philip Butler (Vietnam POW)*

Lesson 57

When is Mediocrity Better than Excellence?

Simple. When mediocrity is acted upon and excellence is left undone.

A mediocre idea acted on has 100 times the chance for success than the great idea left buried. That is why mediocre people often succeed when over talented people don't. The person of mediocre talent who is successful has more fortitude, more drive. He has to prove himself because his talent is not necessarily equal to what he wishes.

If you have an excellent idea, don't accept that it will work just because it is brilliant: work on it, push it. You need the drive and desire to push. Leaving it as a good idea will allow it to die. If you are afraid of failing with this idea consider this, if you don't attempt it you have already failed. By not attempting something you have failed at the attempt. Take your idea and form a plan for its success. Then get up and follow that plan through. Don't run it through in your mind a thousand times, because all the possible outcomes you may dream of may not ever come to fruition. It's the experience you gain from attempting that pushes you to the caliber of achieving. Become a doer. Take any idea you have now and give it a push.

A great idea is worthless unless the drive to see it through is present.

He that can't endure the bad
Will not live to see the good.

—Yiddish proverb

Endurance is one of the most difficult disciplines,
But it is to the one who endures
That final victory comes.

—Buddha

Lesson 58

Write Your Eulogy Today

I know this sounds morbid, but do it. Write down: Here lays John...
And say whatever will be said about you. What would be the highlights
of your life? What would be your greatest achievement? What would
people remember you for? And, what have you left behind? Have you
left the world a better place than you found it? Have you touched at
least one person's life through your presence on this earth? These are
serious things to think about. If you're not happy with what you say or
hear, change it. This is only a practice eulogy. There is an opportunity
to re-write it. Maybe you should write one every year. Think of the goals
that you want to achieve and have never tried. Think of the beautiful
things you wanted to say to your spouse or child and never did. Step
back away from the podium from where you are delivering your eulogy
and change what you do not like.

The goals you will want to achieve and strive for lie in the principles
of the wind. But the perseverance with which you strive to attain these
goals is fire principle. You must understand that in delivering this
eulogy that you still have a chance to achieve your goals before it is too
late.

Imagine if you were lying in a hospital bed with a death sentence.
Then suddenly someone came to you with a cure for your disease.

Certainly you would live life with more vitality than you had before. You would certainly see that many of the things with which you were needlessly concerned were futile. Why does it take a catastrophic occurrence to change one's life? Why not just change it now because we can? By taking this exercise seriously, you may just come to understand the meaning behind what you are currently doing. You may look at life with more vigor, more passion.

When you find the things you want to accomplish, write them down. Look for the goals you want to achieve in the next 10 years. Break these goals into actions you can follow on a daily basis in order to achieve your them. Examine them carefully. If your goal is to own your own house, you need to consider a down payment, as well as a monthly income that will substantiate a mortgage payment. Maybe you need to get a part time job, or work harder on the job you have. Maybe you need to work an extra hour a day. Whatever it takes, write it down and put that thought into action.

The actions you will take now, no matter how small, will reward you ten-fold in the future.
If a man hasn't discovered something that he will die for,
He isn't fit to live.
—Martin Luther King Jr.
This is the story of the Japanese warrior Nobunaga. One battle he waged found him against an enemy consisting of ten times the number of soldiers. His soldiers didn't share his enthusiasm for victory. On the way to the battle he stopped at a shrine and went in for prayer. He came out a while later and told his men, "Let destiny guide us, I will take this coin and toss it into the air. If it lands heads, we will win, tails we will lose." He tossed the coin. Heads came up. All the soldiers were now filled with enthusiasm and motivation. The battle was won easily.

After the battle, Nobunaga's assistant said to him, "Nothing can change the hand of destiny." Nobunaga replied, "You are correct." He then handed him the coin, heads on both sides.

Lesson 59

Goals

The power of goals lies in the element of wind. Goals are of the element of air. They are void of any concrete existence but once materialized, they can be felt. You can feel the wind blowing through your hair although you can't see it. Others can see your hair standing up, but can't see the wind either. The result of the wind is all that is visible. The same holds true with your goals, until they are accomplished they are as void of form as the wind itself. It takes a great deal of focus to materialize something from form to reality. To materialize them we must take several steps.

In attaining a goal we must remain flexible to change. There is a story, it goes like this:

There were two trees, an oak and a willow. They lived happily next to each other, even though the oak overshadowed the willow. A bad storm arose one day. Both of the trees just wanted to survive the storm. The longer the wind blew the stronger the oak tried to stand up, and remain erect to fight back the wind. Contrarily, the willow remained flexible and bent gently with the wind. Finally the wind grew so strong that the oak could not stand it any more and snapped. The willow continued to bend. At the end of the storm only one of the two trees' goal had been met. Strength doesn't necessarily add up the way we imagine.

A person who is open to change is not the weaker one; he might even be considered the stronger since his demeanor is so that it will survive under a variety of conditions. In order to attain goals we must remain flexible. Things in life are bound to change. Just when you have the best plan laid out, something comes along and throws you for a curve. The flexibility you learn from the wind principle allows you to conquer all obstacles, even those that are unforeseen.

I give you this example of the relationship between the element of the wind and goals merely as a reference, as with all the other elements noted in this book. Keep in mind that throughout all of the chapters I have, and will continue to compile examples from one element and another to make points.

I would like you to understand one thing when it comes to goals and their relation to the wind. The wind is always changing, as should be our goals. That is to say, once we accomplish our goal, we must set a new one. Nothing can be worse than a person who accomplishes a goal and then is complacent in that accomplishment. I have always had a great way for dealing with the achievement of goals. Once I saw that my goal was within reach I would push it out of reach by resetting the goal. This allows me to see that I have come to the point of my goal where it would be accomplished, but I must continue to strive for more and more.

If this works for you, then use it. Keep your goals just out of reach. Keep striving for more. Don't allow the demon of complacency to slay you.

Lesson 60

Setting Goals Is Equally As Important As Achieving Them

No goal in the world can be achieved unless it is first set. There are many methods for setting goals, which is what I will address here. Setting goals is, similar to making a business plan. Examine exactly what it is you desire and why. Spend a great deal of time on why, this is the most important part. What is it about achieving this goal that drives you. What does the outcome mean to you? If the outcome is money, why is the money so important to you? What will you do with the money you gain? Write down on a piece of paper the goal you have and underneath your reasons for wanting to achieve this goal. I will stress that a goal of money is a goal that will be void of any meaning unless you have a specific use and reason for the money. Just to achieve a goal of having a million dollars is void of substance. What will you do with the money? Will you make someone's life easier? Will you buy a house for yourself and your family? Be clear on what you desire.

Write your goals down on a piece of paper, do it now. Write it down in exact detail. Draw pictures if necessary or clip some out of a magazine and paste them next to the written goal. This will aid you in visualization. A person who decides not to write a goal down is afraid to fail and therefore probably will. Put your thoughts on paper. When they are on paper you can reflect back on them over and over. They become like a map to guide you along your path to attaining them.

Now that the goal and the reason the goal is important to you are on a piece of paper so that we can see it often and study it, we need to develop a strategy. This will be the active part of conquering the goal at hand, the road map so to speak. Each goal must have a series of steps that you can take to achieve it. Since goals generally are not accomplished in just one step, we must look at how to lay out the groundwork. Just a quick note here, if the goal can be achieved in one step it is not really much of a goal, but rather a step you should take anyway.

> *Whatever things you desire, when you pray,*
> *Believe that you possess them,*
> *And you shall have them.*
>
> *—Mark 11:24*

Break your goal into a series of steps.

The first step:

Understanding- Clearly understanding what your goal is. Define the limitations and boundaries of your goal. Understand why this goal is important to you and why it drives you. Understand the outcome of this goal for better or worse. Define both the positive and negative effects of the outcome of this goal. In that I mean *what will happen if I meet this goal and what will happen if I don't meet this goal?* You need to be psychologically tied to the outcome of this goal.

This is the initial phase of your attack. This phase lies in the planning stage, the assessment of what we desire. Where is the goal with relation to where I am now?

Second step:

Visualization- Meditate and visualize on this goal. See it in your mind. See yourself doing what it is that this goal is. Visualization is the most powerful tool. If you can't imagine yourself having completed this goal, chances are you won't. If this is the case, you must gather more resources on the subject of your goal. Read more about it, look at more pictures, and talk to more people. Set aside 15 minutes each day thinking about the positive outcome of this goal. Imagine yourself with the new car, the mate of your dreams, in the position you want at work. Whatever this goal is, imagine yourself during these 15 minutes having achieved your goal.

Third step:

Requirements- What is necessary to achieve this goal? Education, relationships, hard work, contacts, exercise, etc. List the requirements for the attainment of your goal. Know exactly what it is you need to do. If your goal is a promotion, and for that promotion you need a certain additional degree or certificate, write that down. If your goal is to lose weight or bulk up, one requirement might be to spend some time exercising or joining a gym. You might need some workout clothes, a private trainer or books and videotapes on the subject. If you want to write a book about bike riders, you'll need to learn a bit about biking. Anything that is required to attain your goal goes down on your piece of paper. Remember, if necessary add more requirements as you learn about them.

Fourth step:

Sacrifice- What might I need to give up to achieve this goal? This goes along with requirements. As an example, if you want to reduce your body-fat from 18% to 12% you'll probably want to start with diet and exercise. You'll need to sacrifice heavy foods, especially late at night. You'll need to sacrifice going out for beers with the guys and run a mile or two instead. Whether it is time, habits, food or materials know what you need to give up and give it up. Understand that nothing that is worthwhile will be achieved without some degree of sacrifice.

I remember reading about a point Arnold Schwarzenegger made a long time ago. He stated that if you would sacrifice just one hour of sleep a night, imagine what you could accomplish. You could learn a language in the period of a year. I applied this to some of my clients who had a problem finding time to workout due to a poor scheduling. I should actually say poor planning, since exercise must be important enough in your life to fit it in irrespective of your work schedule. Anyway, I asked these clients to set their alarm clock just 20 minutes earlier in order to allow time for exercise. I told them to go to a quiet place in the house and stretch for the 20 minutes they had gained in their day. After six months none of them complained about the loss of sleep, but all of them were amazed at the amount of progress they made in flexibility.

Fifth Step:

Practice- Practice acting the part. If your goal is to be 15 pounds lighter, act like it. Dress proud like you will dress when you achieve your goal. Wear the nicest clothes you have, groom yourself. Take pride in yourself while you are achieving your goal. Practice talking to people like you will talk to them when you are their manager. Practice looking for cars like you will when you have your $100,000.

Sixth Step:

Time limit- It is crucial that you set a time limit to accomplish the task at hand. Why you ask? Because a goal that does not have a time limit is left up in the air until it is accomplished whenever, *if ever.* You need to set a concrete date on which you will realize your goal. Be definitive on this date. Pick a realistic amount of time it will take you to achieve this goal and write it down. Many people do not like to write down a specific time because they fear that they may not be able to come in on schedule. Time schedules are important in daily life. If you think about it almost everything in your life runs on a schedule—daylight, work, seasons, traffic lights, even your life. Imagine what the world would be like if everything were just left to arbitrary time frames; if the traffic light just changed *whenever,* if the plane would land *sometime later today,* if you could go home *later.*

This discipline is important in the order of things and is important in your order of goal achievement. Although I stress the importance of timeframes, don't give up if you don't come in on time. As you see your deadline approaching you must push yourself, as you should have been doing all along. The deadline is approaching yet you are still off on your goal. Now what? Simple, if the deadline arrives before the completion of the goal, set a new deadline. You will be more likely to judge what a realistic deadline is once you have practiced meeting a few goals.

Seventh Step:

Interaction- Talk to people who have already achieved this goal in their lives, or people who have achieved similar goals. You will learn a lot from people who understand what it is you are trying to achieve. These people will generally be more than willing to help you if they are approached properly, if not, you probably would never learn anything form them anyway. Surrounding yourself with the people of similar mind will ease your way. Like minded people will be prone to help one another whether it is through support or actions.

If these people are unavailable to you, form what Dale Carnegie called an "Invisible Committee". These are the people that either have already accomplished your goal or are in the process of accomplishing it. The important thing in surrounding yourself with others is that these people must share your enthusiasm and vigor. Negative energy will squash your goal fast. If anyone you are around is negative to the accomplishment of your goal, cut him or her out of the loop. Your day to day challenges will be difficult enough without negative influences.

Eighth Step:

Realization- In your daily life see yourself having achieved your goal. As long as you are on the journey to accomplishing this goal you are in fact accomplishing it. See yourself in the act of the goal's completion. People whose goal it is to lose 10 pounds are on the way to that goal once they've lost their first pound. You must understand this fully. Reward yourself for starting and continuing this process. Many people wait till the end to see that they are accomplishing the goal.

The thousand-mile journey begins with a single step.

Bear in mind the fact that the first step is as important to the thousand-mile journey as the last.

Ninth Step:

Actualization- By actualization, I mean that at this point your goal is accomplished. In the past I have set goals and put the proper focus on them but not kept track of them. Before I knew it I had already accomplished the goal. Some people who are looking to lose weight get past the initial hump of exercise and dieting and before they know it, they have surpassed their goal and they keep going. People often learn to enjoy the things that were once considered *tasks* in the accomplishment of their goals. These actions are now part of their daily lives and benefit them greatly in achievement of other goals and enriching their lives.

Lesson 61

Create A Goal Book

A valuable tool that I love to use is a goal book. In it I write down my goals and their parameters. I write down the steps that I take to see that goal through; I note the date of conception, the date of projected completion and the date of accomplishment. If I however have pushed my goal a step further, then I write that down in my book also.

Example:

Date: 1/1/99

Goal: To increase income by $1000.00 per month

Date of projected completion: 7/1/99

If by 6/15/99 I have already increased my income by $950.00, then I place an asterisk (*) next to goal in my book and modify it as follows.

*Date: 6/15/99

Goal: To increase income by $1400.00 per month

Date of projected completion: 12/1/99

Pursuing this technique will keep you constantly reaching to achieve more, yet allow you the chance to see the actualization of you goals.

By using the tools of realization and actualization together you will find that you have accomplished your goal while you are still in the process.

Using a goal book gives me the opportunity to reflect back on past accomplishments and use insights I've gained, insights that I might otherwise overlook. I am often amazed at, **that what I am now doing was once a goal of mine.** I also remind myself, the life I am living is not an accident, it is the result of my previous efforts.

> *You must have long range goals*
> *To keep you from being frustrated by short-range failures*
> *—Charles C. Noble*
> *Set short term goals and you'll win games.*
> *Set long term goals and you'll win championships.*
> *—Anonymous*

Lesson 62

Flexibility

Just like the muscle that is not stretched before training, the attitude that is not flexible will snap at the first sign of stress.

Wind and air are the most flexible of elements. The other element that is extremely flexible that I address in this book is water. I will discuss that in the *Overcoming Obstacles Chapter*. If you think of the element of air, which comprises wind, it can take any shape. Wind can pass through a wide canyon and also through a narrow doorway. Wind blows equally as strong against a straw house and against a brick building. Remember also that wind changes direction faster than anything else. Wind never changes based on the strength of the opponent. If the wind is blowing against a twig it will blow equally as hard as if it were blowing against a giant redwood tree. We should adopt this attitude. Any obstacle we encounter while trying to achieve our goal must be met with countering energy.

I must stress that it is important to know your opinions and goals and why you have them. *Just because* is not good enough. If your opinion is of a serious nature, explain it in detail and it certainly will be accepted and respected. If it is not, be flexible to change.

Flexibility has afforded me so many wonderful things. The meaning behind the wind principle is the opportunity for new things that are right in front of us. Many times a person who does not want to go on a particular business trip ends up going and falling in love with the city they are in. Or closing the biggest deal of their career. Whatever it might be standing in the way of your goal observe it and learn from it.

When I was in my twenties I dated a girl from Switzerland. At that time I was working as a bodyguard earning a six-figure income. I decided to quit my job and move to Switzerland and live with her. When I got there, she broke up with me and was already dating someone else. Of course I was angry and hurt. I didn't know what to do. I stayed with a student of mine and began teaching karate there as a way of keeping my mind occupied. Needless to say, I didn't have much to come home to since my career had now taken a big change. I had made my decision to quit bodyguarding and I wasn't going to change my mind back again. I looked at this setback as an opportunity. I met wonderful people in Switzerland and stayed there for quite some time. Erich (my student there) trained with me almost everyday, trading ski lessons for karate classes. I became an avid skier. He became a black belt. He opened his own school and now has many students that are probably grateful that this girl dumped me. I came back to the states and opened a school in Los Angeles. Through this decision, I have met so many new wonderful people including the people that convinced me to write this book. In the heart of this turmoil I was able to understand that there was an opportunity for growth even though I couldn't see it at that point.

My goal was to grow from my bodyguarding experience and open myself up to new horizons. My goals were simple and pure. I never, in a million years, thought that the realization of my goals would be as rewarding as it has turned out to be. My flexibility was very evident to me. Somewhere out there, there is a plan. I can influence it, but I must leave room for divine intervention. I can work and work at a goal, but if it is not meant to be, it may not be. If I give it all I've got and it doesn't go, I back up, regroup and try again from a different angle. I remember the lessons from the previous try. If it still doesn't work, I ask questions and reassess. Most of the time I find, at this point, that what I am trying to do *is not* necessary and there *is* another way around it.

It is often better to have a great deal of harm happen to one than a little;
A great deal may rouse you to remove what a little will only accustom
you to endure.
—*Grenville Kleiser*

Noble souls, through dust and heat,
Rise from disaster and defeat the stronger.
—**Henry Wadsworth Longfellow**

Lesson 63

Money

Many people set their goals to be the accumulation of money. I consider this a waste of a perfectly good goal. Remember that your goals need to be concrete, money is an abstract. Money is only good for what it can buy; money in and of itself is useless. Do not spend much of your efforts on something that is merely an abstract concept. Do not confuse the concept of money as the possession of wealth.

One of the most fascinating concepts of all is that of money as wealth. If I asked you to describe a wealthy man to me I'm certain that the first thing that would come to your mind would be a person's monetary standing. I would like to tell you that this is not true. To equate money to wealth is ridiculous. Money has as much to do with wealth, as tomatoes have to do with pineapple juice. Wealth is money spent. Wealth is happiness. A rich man is one who is happy with that which he has. Money is a tool. It can be used to buy things that give people a good feeling. The true symbol of the wealth that money represents is the gold that is locked away in the vaults, this gold is the true value. Our currency does not contain this precious metal. Coins are made of cheap alloys and bills are made from paper and cloth. A true example of this is confederate money. This money was so useless that its greatest value was the warmth it generated in the oven on cold evenings after its devaluation. Millions of dollars were stocked away for that rainy day that never came. Imagine how much happiness was denied because of the concept of "accumulation". Moneys value lies in spending it, using this valueless substance to acquire things of need.

If I am the greatest teacher of martial arts alive but instead I choose to work as an investment banker because the financial rewards are better, what good is the wealth of my knowledge? In my career as a bodyguard, a tremendous amount of responsibility and expertise were involved. Most people who worked with me and for me, were almost double my age at that time. It was a career that I was able to maintain due to my training. The money I was paid was high. With this money I was able to buy nice clothes, take great vacations, eat in fancy restaurants, and save money. Many years later I decided to stop working as a bodyguard. I quit my job, packed up my things and moved to Europe. I had no job there, I just went. I was able to maintain a lifestyle there by teaching martial arts. Upon coming back to the states I realized, I had taught myself a great lesson. By removing myself from this career I saw a need to fulfill something else in my life. I found it necessary to teach, to bring myself to others through the martial arts. I wanted to teach others my style and ideas. When the time seemed right I took all the money I had left, and some I borrowed, and I opened a dojo. This was not meant to be a profitable venture, at least not monetarily. You see I had already experienced monetary wealth. At this state I wanted something more. I realized by doing this that I am wealthier now than I had ever been before. My income during my karate teaching days was much less than it many other business ventures, but I still found the resources to buy clothes, go out to eat take care of and whatever else may arise. I got up in the morning, have breakfast, workout, and go to the office. I would handle my office duties during the day; teach a few classes and was 100% confident that I could not have been wealthier. I had a job that I would do for free. I was the envy of many people I know. My point is not that everyone should go out and open a dojo, quite the contrary; everyone should find happiness in what they are doing. It is important that you are happy, what you do must appeal to you. If you enjoy math, a great career could be teaching math or working in accounting. There are many careers for each person's likes.

There should be absolutely no reason for anyone to be unhappy in his or her lives.

happiness = wealth
this is one of the greatest untruths that exists

I found out that the money I had in reserve was merely a tool. Something I needed to get rid of to attain wealth. What is in the past could only help me if I could utilize it in the present.

All animals except man
Know that the principle business of life
Is to enjoy it.

—*Samuel Bulter*

If I am walking on a beach right now and suddenly were to be swept away by the hand of G-d the only footprints I wish to leave behind are the ones I am standing in now. It is what I am currently accomplishing that is important. I use the experience of all my past lessons as tools in making today my best day ever.

He that is of a merry heart
Hath a continual feast.

—*Proverbs 15:15*

Man's real life is happy,
Chiefly because he is ever expecting
That it soon will be so.

—*Edgar Allan Poe*

Lesson 64

Focus On The Big Picture

Don't focus on the most prosperous outcome,
Focus on the outcome that will be best.

Focusing on the outcome that will net you the highest profit or most prestige can result in negative karma in other areas of your life. This concept has led me to a better understanding why some people can be so successful in one area of their lives, yet fail miserably in others.

A friend of mine told me a story about a man who wanted to become very successful. He was offered numerous jobs because of his people skills and sales ability. The job he accepted was the one that promised the most pay, a job selling bombs and bomb-making materials. Everything was great in his family and career. He had a wonderful family and plenty of money. He owned a nice house and enjoyed the luxury of an upper class income. He was near the top of his company in sales and received many bonuses and accommodations at work. As the result of his efforts as a successful salesman many innocent people lost their lives.

A healthy man all through his life, suddenly a bomb of another sort went off in his life. Without any warning one day he was diagnosed with cancer. He suffered immensely physically and emotionally, as did his family until he eventually died riddled with the disease. Could this result have been due to a karmic repayment? A payback for the suffering and pain that others experienced through his gains?

Provision for others is a fundamental responsibility of human life.
—*Woodrow Wilson*

Could a person who loves any one thing too much be punished by it or as a result of it? Could the Taoist principle of not clinging to an ideal or thought too tightly have some significance in our daily lives? The story goes something like this:

The young monk went to the river and saw the reflection of the moon in the water. He looked to see if no one was watching. When the coast was clear, he crashed his hands into the water to steal the moon. He looked into his hands to see that the moon had vanished from both his hands and the river. Puzzled, he looked around as well as up to the moon. Upon looking back to the river he noticed the moon had re-appeared. Again he tried to snatch the moon, again losing it both in his hands as well as the river. The master came out from beside the tree and smiled. "If you desire the moon, gently embrace it in your hands and it will stay with you." The young monk followed the advice and noticed that the moon not only was in his hands, but also remained in the river for others to experience.

Focusing on the overall picture gives you a clear edge. Be focused and clear about your desires. Do not let your life become a tunnel, where if you do not attain that certain goal nothing else matters.

If necessary, be prepared to walk away. Nothing in the world is worth everything. You must be ready to walk away from anything or any person if necessary.

Don't love anything too much, don't cling to anything too tightly.

Lesson 65

The Quality of Quality

Nothing that is too good is truly too good

For the numerous sales objections of "it's too expensive" I have used the analogy of cost vs. value. It is something that I believe so strongly in that it makes it easy for me to overcome this objection. I never hesitate to spend more on something that is of superior value. If it is of superior value, it truly doesn't cost more, it just has a higher value.

If you can't afford to buy the best, save up. Whatever you have should be the best.

It is important to note that to have the very best in things implies not always having a lot of things. I have seen many people's houses, people of modest means, and being truly impressed by their possessions. They were carefully thought out and of very high quality.

In my opinion, it is better to have a few good things, than a lot of ok things.

In the days of the Samurai, the warriors would pride themselves on one possession, the katana/long sword. Equally, the sword-makers would pride themselves on the quality of the work they invested in this sword. Most warriors would travel the land and carry most of their possessions with them.

Think of something that you lay immense pride in and decide to get the one that is the best you can afford. Be it your car, your watch, your house, whatever. Be aware, I said the best you can afford. Don't go broke to prove a point. The best you can afford will give you an immense sense of pride that will shine through in everything you do.

If there is something that you want, study it first. Do research and realize that you may have this possession for a long time. Do not be limited by the price of an item, be realistic and sincere. If it is a car you are looking for, don't look at a $100,000 car and fool yourself in believing it is the best car for you. What is important to determine is what makes it best for you. Your needs may not necessitate a car that does 0-60 in 5.7 seconds with a top speed of 200 mph. Once you have been honest enough with yourself about what you need and why, you will be of a clear mind to move forward. Now deal with the price issue. Negotiate and deal to the best of your ability. If you take this attitude, you have a clear conscience about the decision you have made. It will also free up your mind for more important decisions.

> *The first rule (of becoming wealthy) is not to lose money.*
> *The second rule is not to forget the first rule.*
> —*Warren Buffet*

A friend of mine who just happens to be a millionaire related this story to me. He was working in his office one day and his copy machine broke. It had been on the fritz for several months but members of his staff had not said anything to him. On this particular day he made it to the copy-room to photocopy something and noticed that the machine made very poor quality copies. He asked his assistant about it and the girl replied, oh yes, just slam this here and then push this and it will work. He told me this was too much effort for his mind to be occupied with. He just wanted to push a button and make copies. He walked back to his office and called the local Canon Copier salesman. He told him the model he had and the problem he faced. The salesman said he could have the repairman there by the end of the week. "Well how fast can you have a new machine here for me?" he asked. "In the next four hours." The salesman replied. "Ok fine send me over the best model you have that will fit in the room." Just like that, he solved his problem. I asked him how much this cost him and he said about $30,000. I thought this was a lot of money. He said it was for that day, "But now my mind is free to make million dollar deals again, and my employees can spend their time working and not fixing a broken copy machine."

If you have a problem that money can fix, and you have the money, you don't have a problem.

Lesson 66

The Warrior Burns His Bridges Behind Him

This concept is different than that of burning ones bridges with people. In burning your bridges here, I mean to allow yourself no room for failure or retreat. The general who led his army into the village and burned the bridges once the troops had crossed them forced his soldiers to focus, there was no way out, no escape. They had to win. Take this attitude in everything you do. How many times do you hear someone tell you of their ultimate goal and then follow it up with, "But if that doesn't work, then I'll…." What is that supposed to mean? What it means to me is that the person is not serious about the goal of which they speak, they don't have the mind of the warrior. To the warrior there is no way out, but to win. Burning your bridges means not giving yourself that cushion of a way out. It is all or nothing. Look at your life, your career and your goals like this and you will immerge victorious.

> *Nothing great will ever be achieved without great men,*
> *And men are great only if they are determined to be so.*
> *—Charles de Gaulle*

I have approached so much of my life in this fashion. It has been by being a doer my whole life that I have been able to succeed. My entire life people have told me that I couldn't do a particular thing, I used that as motivation to show them. Many times I had expressed my desires to a so-called friend only to hear them say, "But Robert, what if that doesn't work?" My answer always was, "There is no room for failure in my life." I don't understand the people who have a failure mentality. Negativity is not allowed in my life. If it comes in, I deal with it and demolish it. I once went to this therapist, I stress *once*. Her evaluation after 30 minutes of counseling was, "Robert, you can't live your life and not deal with negativity, you have to face it here." I thanked her and left. I told her that this would be a negative experience for me and I have no place for it in my life. My life has been just fine since then. Sure negative things have come into my life, but I have destroyed them and overcome them just as fast as they came in.

If you can get negative things out of your life, do it now.
Negativity clutters the mind's ability to achieve positive results.
I've never seen a monument erected to a pessimist.
—Paul Harvey

Achieving Mastery the Element of the Void

This is the most complex issue to try and explain. The person who masters himself, masters the universe. The element associated with self-mastery is the void, which is absolute nothingness. One cannot attain any self-mastery if he holds on to preconceptions, prejudices, anger, hostility, fear or ignorance. The master holds on to nothing unimportant.

In order to understand the element of the void, you must have a basic understanding of Zen. In a parable a student was to imagine the sound of one hand clapping. The master told the student to go and mediate on the sound of one hand clapping. For days the student was bewildered, how one hand could clap. He questioned the Koan/parable over and over, until his enlightenment he then realized the sound of one hand clapping was the sound of no sound, the sound of silence.

The worst loneliness is not to be comfortable with yourself.

—*Mark Twain*

In letting go of the ego/the self we learn to accept things as they are. But we cannot accept things as they are until we let go of all the junk that rumbles in our heads and hearts. I hope you have not just opened the book to this page to start reading because this is the only section of the book you will not understand until you have understood the rest of this book.

The great warriors were trained in battle from the times they were children. Sword fighting was second nature to them. They did not have to think how to move or parry a strike, it just happened. Their bodies had a mind of their own so-to-speak. The master of any art does his craft without much thought. In fact to truly master a craft it must just happen. The painting must appear as a result of putting the brush into your hand. The clay must form itself; the words must appear on the page…

Understanding this section is sort of similar to bicycle riding. First you learn with the training wheels. When the training wheels are taken off you focus on keeping your balance, looking forward, pedaling, steering, etc. But once you understand the balance and feel the balance, you let go of it. You don't think about balance when you get on the bicycle after you have been *riding for a while, instead you think of the ride. The balancing part is second nature. So too will be the elements and principles in this book. Once you are on the road to mastering the art of success, success will just happen. You will be utilizing the tools in this book without thought, they must become a second nature. They must be a part of your everyday life. We do not think about eating, we simply eat when we are hungry, we sleep when we are tired and so on and so on.*

Mastering the art of success is making successful thinking a part of our lives. Once we take these steps, we are on the road to success.

If people are suffering,
They must look within themselves…
Happiness is not something ready-made [Buddha] can give you.
It comes from your own actions.

—The Dalai Lama

Lesson 67

The Two Zen Priests

On their daily walk, two Zen priests shared stories with one another. They had been friends for many years and had shared many a walk together. Coming upon the river they noticed a beautiful young girl attempting to cross, but fearful of getting wet. The first priest noticed her, he walked over and picked her up and carried her across the river. Once on the other side the girl thanked him and went on her way. The second priest continued his conversation with the first as they continued to walk along in stride. After several hours the second priest looked at the first and said, "You know, I have to tell you that I am quite bothered by something." Really? What is it?" Asked the first. "Well you know that we are not supposed to have any interaction with women." "Yes, I understand," replied the first. "Well, a few hours ago, back at the river, you picked up and carried that beautiful girl across the water." The first priest replied, "Yes, you're absolutely right, but what's amazing to me is the fact that I left her back there at the river, and you, you are still carrying her."

The message in this little story is that you can carry, in your conscience, problems that don't exist any more in your life. Carrying problems is self-limiting. You must learn to let go of things that are in the past, you either have solved the problem, or it has gone unsolved. In either case, it is in the past. Continuing to deal with them puts a burden on your daily load. The issues that you have to deal with today are enough without adding to them things you should have let go of yesterday, last week or even last year. The person who is at peace with himself and his surroundings is the master of the self.

If you have a garden filled with daisies and wish to grow roses, you have to first remove the daisies. You can't expect the soil or space to accommodate both flowers. The roses will demand all of your attention, so will your mind. Only the person who will give up his or her baggage will be able to grow. In order to expand your horizons you have to be certain that you are clear with your present state. The only way to move ahead is to be completely content with where you are now. To move ahead means to move on from where you stand. You will not be able to do this if you are not free of the concerns that burden you.

Of course I understand that this may be easier said than done, but you must try. No matter how traumatic an experience, try to understand that you are giving that experience the power to continue to limit you in the future until you *let it go*. If the experience left an emotional scar on you, you may consider counseling in order to better deal with the problem. There is nothing to be ashamed of to seek professional help. It merely shows you are a stronger person than the person who chooses to ignore it. In the mean time, there is a quote that I feel will help you. It is by the father of positive thinking, Dr. Norman Vincent Peale. He says when you find yourself in a place where you feel hopeless, repeat the following affirmation to yourself. It has worked for me and I know it will work for you regardless of your faith. Here is the affirmation:

I can do all things through G-d, who strengthens me.

Lesson 68

The Cup

A student went to the master to study. Upon arriving all the student could think about was getting started with the exercises and techniques. The master came out from the back room and looked at the young man. "Would you like a cup of tea," asked the master. "Yeah, sure," the young man replied. The master handed the student a cup and poured his cup full, and continued to pour until the cup overflowed all over the floor. "Stop," the young man said, "my cup is already full". The master looked at him and said, "Go, please, and come back when your cup is empty."

The truth in this story is that we can not learn something if we have a preconceived idea about it. When a new student comes to my dojo I always ask about their fighting experience. Nothing is more challenging than teaching the person with a moderate amount of knowledge. It is these students that will not let go of their ideas and make it much more difficult for me to teach them. The people who have attained a degree of proficiency in another style usually will let go of what they have learned temporarily and will absorb what it is that I am attempting to teach them. To me, the best student is the one without prior experience or a desire to fight. These students generally make very good martial artists. They have no ego and nothing to prove.

This relates so clearly to business that it should be taught in the first year of every MBA program. If you come to the table expecting anything, you are full of preconceptions. Preconceptions will destroy you. It is good to make plans, it is good to follow plans, it is however imperative to know how to deal with life when plans fall through.

Henry Ford knew this when he was in the process of inventing the V8 engine. His team of engineers continuously came to him and told him that it will never work. All Mr. Ford could say was try again. He simply had no preconception of why it could not work, he only knew there was a way. Previous knowledge and experience limited his engineers. Ford was void of knowledge and experience that could limit him. Empty your cup of preconceptions and experiences when you enter a new situation. Understand that each new experience will allow you a new set of experiences. Come to the table ready to experience, ready to learn, ready to grow.

There is no happiness except in the realization
That we have accomplished something.

—Henry Ford

Lesson 69

It's in the Blood

There is a family of martial artists that has come to the US and under their name won more "Bare Knuckle" fights than anyone. They began teaching their art and many people flocked to their schools. Many of these people became very good fighters, but none could match anyone in the family. Why? Simple, these boys were raised on the mat, fighting was in their blood. From the day they were old enough to crawl Dad threw them around and taught them, there just was no other way.

A similar story is the how the Ninja were able to do the miracles they perform. The ninja were the secret warriors of Japan. They were reputed as the greatest warriors of all times. Among their accomplishments was the ability to be able to hold their breath for extended duration, jump and leap enormous distances and control bodily functions at will. To be a ninja, you were chosen. Ninja were not recruited in their teens; they were recruited in their first months of life. A baby born to a ninja family was trained daily. Their young limbs were contorted and exercised until they could do extraordinary things. Every day of their young lives was spent overcoming obstacles.

With any of these warriors skills are in the blood. It's not about undertaking something today and hopefully succeeding at it in a few months, it is about doing something for your entire life and knowing nothing else. It is about understanding the self through knowing.

You must take this lesson seriously. You must therefore draw on the expertise that you have gained throughout your years. Everything that you have done up to this point has made you the person you are. You will never go into a field of work in which you have no "experience".

In example, if you are a salesperson and are changing careers to become a lawyer, you will draw on you people skills as well as your negotiating skills. Everything that you have done and experienced in your career as a salesperson will make you a stronger lawyer. Once any skill is "in your blood" it will not just leave. The passion and vigor will carry over no matter how far removed your new career might be.

> *Men are wise in proportion not to their experience,*
> *But to their capacity for experience.*
> —*Samuel Johnson*

Lesson 70

Understanding Love

Love is a perfect analogy of the void. Something that cannot be seen, heard, touched or tasted. Yet when experienced it heightens all of these senses.

Anyone who is a master of himself or herself is a person who experiences love. Achieving the greatest things in the world without experiencing love is as empty as a black hole. Of all the achievements that I have ever accomplished, experiencing love and continuing to be able to experience love is certainly my greatest. If I would lose everything I own, everything I stood for, I would not flinch if I were assured that I could have love. Without love I would surely die. Before you use the word love as so many people do, I would like to invite you to truly look at the concept of love.

It seems the simplest things are the most complex to explain. Some things do not need to be explained, they should however be experienced. Love is a word that is so often misunderstood and also misused. In explaining my concept of love I hope it will make sense to you. I also hope it will awaken some of your own feelings of love. If my words can do this I will be extremely happy and will consider my labor of writing this book worthwhile.

I love my girlfriend, I love my parents, I love my students, I love my friends, I love G-d and I love myself. Most of these, I'm certain you understand. I think, however, that you will look at the last of these loves, self-love, as a sort of self centered, egotistical self-serving love. Quite the contrary: I would like to focus on this self love since I feel this is the most important of them all. To love yourself makes you a complete person. People who do not love themselves are empty and incomplete; they are looking for someone or something to give them the love they deny themselves. Why would anyone want to give you something that you deny yourself?

If for example you were an inventor, and developed a product that you wished to show to a group of investors, wouldn't it be easier to gain the confidence and trust of the investors if you believe in the product yourself. It is easy to see that people will be a part of love, but no one will contribute to love where none exists. Self-love is different from conceit. People who are conceited are insecure; they are void of love and are void of the understanding of love. Self-love will build up reserves of love, love that can be given away. Therefore, if you do not have self-love and you meet someone that you wish to experience love with, how will you be able to? You cannot share something that you do not posses, something of which you have no experience. This concept is deeper than the "*feel good about yourself*" ideas that are currently circulating. True self-love allows you to experience yourself fully, as you should allow others to. What's so great about me? What can I offer if I do not love?

Love can never be taken; it can only be given.
Love can never be bought or traded it can only be given.
Love can never be stolen or held hostage, it can only be given.
Love cannot be borrowed or lent or hidden, the only way to receive true love is to give it away.

I am not saying that one should give love for the sole reason of receiving it in return, instead give it to see the joy and happiness you can uncover. Then, you will be able to experience the love that you are giving. To give a donation to a charity is easy, you write the check, lick the stamp, and you're through. However, to give of yourself: your time, energy, effort and heart, these are true gifts.

There once was an old monk who wished to build a temple for his students. The monk solicited donations from villagers, but came up short on cash. The wealthiest resident of the village came to the monk and, in one sum, gave the monk all the money necessary to build the temple. The monk took the money and walked away. Later, the monk's top disciple asked him why he did not give thanks, the monk looked at the student and said, "It is the giver who should give thanks."

The master of success embraces love. He loves his fellow man, he loves his family, he loves himself and he loves what it is he is doing. People are drawn to love and are repelled by hate.

The warrior of love is truly the master of success.

All the special gifts and powers from G-d will someday come to an end,
But love goes on forever...
There are three things that remain—
Faith, hope & love—
And the greatest of these is love.

—Corinthians

Lesson 71

Keep Death Always in Mind
Each Day is A Gift

Life and death are stones on the road; they cannot be avoided. Eternally there is existence. Existence is forever. Our soul is a part of G-d. When we die physically, this part is returned. It again becomes a part of G-d, and apart from what is now us. It separates from us to join its Creator; in essence it leaves the user. Our life, our existence is a loan from the great Creator. It is something we must consider ourselves privileged to have. Life must be honored and respected, not taken for granted. Many people consider it a given that we have life, it is not, it is an honor. What you will do with it is up to you.

Wasting time is wasting life
Wasting life is wasting the greatest gift you were ever given.

Life and death are perfect examples of the void. Life is void of death and death is void of life. We must acknowledge that death is a given. It is said, "No one gets out of this life alive". Now, rather than allowing this thought to paralyze us, let it instead invigorate us. Let it invigorate us in the pursuit of life. Since we know that we are going to die, let us see how much good we can do before that happens. How much *more good* can you do than the person who came before you?

Consider this, if you are 35 years old today and the average person currently lives to be 75, then you have more than half of your life to live, 14,600 days. Break that into hours and it equals 350,400 of which only 2/3 will be waking hours 231,264. Of that you will spend some time driving to and from work, getting ready for work and such, lets say 1.5 hours a day total of 21,900 hours, that leaves you with 209,364. Of that lets say you work an average of 8 hours a day, 5 days a week, approximate total 73,000 hours, remaining 136,364. Your clock, as mine, is ticking. Every day you spend negative, sad or hostile is a day wasted. Nobody can buy more time. This was the essence of the training of the young samurai. The Budoshoshinshu is the warrior's primer, a book over two hundred years old that speaks of the proper upbringing and behavior of the warrior class. The first thing addressed in this book is death. From the time the warrior arises in the morning until he places his head on his pillow to sleep at night death is constantly thought of. This philosophy allows one to respect not only ones own life, but the life of others as well. The fragility with which we all exist is considered and respected. Most importantly, character is improved.

Everything that exists, exists within us. The beautiful stars in the sky, the blooming flower, the smell you love, the sounds that move you, all of these must first exist within us before we can recognize them. A person without an understanding of beauty cannot appreciate a beautiful garden, just as the person without taste can't understand the difference between good and bad wine. The outer experiences are reflections of our innermost sentiments. What we experience outside grows and stays within us forever. It is easy to reflect back on happy and sad thoughts. It is not so easy to remember the ones in the middle. That which does not move us isn't important enough to remember.

One who is in constant touch with death will fully understand the joy and opportunities of life. One who feels the constant joy of life is in understanding with his own self.
One who understands themselves has achieved mastery.
After all, mastery of the self is mastery over the universe.
Though I walk through the valley of the shadow of death
I fear no harm, for You are with me;

—Psalms 23:3

Do you know that disease and death must needs overtake us,
No matter what we are doing?
…What do you wish to be doing when it overtakes you?
…If you have anything better to be doing when you are so overtaken,
Get to work on that.

—Epictetus

Lesson 72

Never Sell a Product...
Represent Yourself

In the days of the samurai loyalty and honor were held in the highest regard. The samurai represented his lord as well as the image of all other samurai. Every move they made, every word they spoke was associated with their affiliates. Therefore bad words were not spoken, good grooming was paramount and loyalty was king.

Try to take this attitude in your daily approach to life. Anyone you are transacting business, or any other deal with, is doing business through you. They are learning as much about you as they are about the person, product and service you represent. It is important to represent yourself and the product or service you are selling from a position of loyalty and honor. More than likely what you represent is available somewhere else at a similar or possibly even a better price, this is why the client must be sold on you first, last and always. You must build the relationship of the two people transacting the deal as more important than the product itself. You symbolize this product in their eyes. Once they believe in you they will want what you are selling. A person selling you health care products would appear unbelievable if he were out of shape, just like nobody wants to go to a doctor who is always sick, a beautician with a bad hairdo or the Mercedes salesman who drives a Lexus.

The personal relationship transcends the business deal and comforts the other side in the transaction. If they are comfortable with your follow-up calls, additional sales and future business is sure to follow. Sell your client on your product and they will look to replace the product when it breaks or runs out, but sell them on you and you have a limitless source of referrals and sales.

> *The most important single ingredient in the formula of success*
> *Is knowing how to get along with people.*
> —*Theodore Roosevelt*

According to Benjamin Franklin there are thirteen virtues necessary for true success. Relate them to yourself and how you deal with others:

Temperance	Silence	Order	Resolution	Frugality
Industry	Sincerity	Justice	Moderation	Cleanliness
Tranquility	Chastity	Humility		

Lesson 73

Don't Judge a Book by its Cover

My sensei (Japanese for teacher) is a funny guy. He heard several upsetting stories about a Cadillac dealer in a Florida town where he lived so he thought it might be funny to play a joke on them. Generally being a fairly well dressed, well-groomed man he decided to slum it for a day. In his sandals, shorts and worn T-shirt he walked in the front door of the Cadillac showroom. He looked around at several of the models, opened and closed the doors, sat in a few and admired them all. Almost 25 minutes had past and the closest thing he got to help was an occasional stare from the sales staff saying as much as to say, "Hey what are you doing in here?"

In walked the newest salesperson of the staff, just returning from lunch. "Hi there" he said eagerly. "Hi to you too" was sensei's reply. "You know these Caddies are some of the most comfortable best riding cars made." Sensei smiled. The young inexperienced salesperson eagerly showed him all the functions and features that he himself was impressed with. Together they chatted and laughed. Almost forgetting the product, the salesperson was selling himself. The salesman, although inexperienced in selling cars, was quite experienced in selling himself. In fact it seemed as though his focus was on building the relationship more than selling the car. But yet to his surprise, sensei had a different agenda. He turned to the salesperson and asked casually, "Hey, what does one of these fancy cars cost?" "Oh they're mighty expensive" replied the salesman. "I sure would love to get one of these for me and my brother," sensei said to the unsuspecting young man. "That is really nice," the salesman replied, "Maybe someday you'll be able to and then I hope you'll come back to me." It was truly the salesman's goal to sell himself rather than his product. Sensei replied, "I will, I promise, but tell me, how much would two of these cost?" "Seventy thousand dollars" was his reply. He looked into his fanny pack, pulled out seventy thousand dollars and said, "Let's make that someday today." He handed the young man the money and made the deal on the spot.

The innocence of the salesperson worked in his favor. In fact it wasn't even innocence, it was purity. A sincere interest in what he was doing and a desire to build a relationship gave him the edge over all the more experienced salespeople in the showroom. All the sales courses, training, bonuses and hype didn't give them the strength that this young man had in people skills. The salesman was not trained in how to spot a "good lead" or how to close a sale. He was simply sincerely interested in this other person (who comes to find out had $70K in his fanny pack). Understanding that everyday is a gift, treat every moment accordingly. Enjoy the moments, the people, and the experiences you have with all of your heart and soul.

Funny, now I hear often that in Beverly Hills, you are more likely to get help in a car dealership, wearing shorts than a suit. Pretentiousness is dying.

Be aware of the guppy that swims around then bites you like a shark.
Those who never retract their opinions
Love themselves more than they love the truth.
—Joseph Joubert

Lesson 74

Man's Mortal Perfection

It is the function of perfection
To make one know one's imperfection.

—*Saint Augustine*

I'm not sure how this story will relate to you but I need to tell it anyway.

There once was a sword-maker that was known for the highest quality swords in all the land. He had a young assistant who looked up to the master in awe. Watching the master painstakingly work on a sword for over a week the student took note of the hundreds of folds the master put into the blade. Each strike with the hammer was precisely placed. Upon finishing the blade the master examined his work. It was perfect. After he finished examining it, he picked up the file and placed a small gouge into the bottom side of it. The student was in shock. "Why did you do that to this perfect blade, it was flawless." "You are right," replied the master, "But remember, only G-d is perfect."

The moral of this story was the sword-maker's fear of perfection. It is my opinion that he was afraid of attaining this "ultimate level" of perfection. If he were to reach the level of "god-like" perfection, he would have nowhere else to go in his mind. So, instead, he puts himself back down to the level of a mortal in his eyes.

Perfection does not exist.
To understand this is the triumph of human intelligence;
To expect to possess it is the most dangerous kind of madness.
—Alfred de Musset

I think this is a wonderful story to bear in mind when we think about our own level of perfection. Although we may try and try for our entire lives to attain perfection in something we strive for, how many of us would be humble enough to pull ourselves back to square one if we actually achieve perfection. The sword-maker had no ego, he was void of self, and it was his intention only to make excellent swords, not to be "perfect".

Remember, no matter how much you try to achieve perfection, you will never attain it. True perfection always lies just out of our reach. The master is content with his journey. He keeps his goals just slightly ahead of his reach. If by chance he reaches that goal, he will again set it, placing it just ahead of his reach.

Strive to achieve your goals, when you reach them set them again.
Always just outside of your reach.

Lesson 75

The Most Valuable Saying

There is an old story about the famous calligrapher Teshu. He was a master at the Japanese art of Shodo (Japanese calligraphy). It was his goal to paint a million pieces in his life. He was commissioned to paint many pieces for some of the richest, most prestigious people in Japan.

One day he was commissioned to paint something for a very wealthy lord. The only request the lord had was that it should be something that would bring happiness to his house. Teshu thought on this for a very long time. Each time the lord would ask for his painting, Teshu replied, "It is not done yet."

Finally after several months Teshu brought the masterpiece to the lord. He unrolled the scroll and presented it.

It read:

Grandfather dies
Father dies
Son dies.

Not knowing what to make of this, the lord accepted. It took him several years to learn the value in this writing, but I hope it will not take you as long to understand it.

Things that happen in natural progression are the things that should bring us the most happiness. The evolution of the family is a beautiful process. If you are a father or mother, you may understand this better than anyone else.

In mastering success we must accept things that are out of our control. We cannot personalize things as "why did this happen to me"? Many people suffer adverse situations in life and still persevere. Learn from your setbacks. Often times the greatest periods of growth come after a setback. If you allow it to hold you back, you are caving to its power, on the other hand, if you triumph, you squash it.

> *Acceptance of things that cannot be changed is very important.*
> *The final redemption is no longer a dream of a distant future,*
> *But an imminent reality.*
> *—The Lubavitcher Rabbi*

Lesson 76

How Long Does it Take to Learn?

Here is a story to illustrate the point of mastery.

Among Teshu's favorite topics to paint was Daruma, the grand patriarch of Zen. He would paint hundreds of paintings of Daruma with his sumie ink and brush weekly. One day a man walked up to him and commented on one particular of Daruma. "Master?" Asked the man, "How long did it take you to paint that painting?" Teshu looked at him and smiled, "20 minutes and 25 years."

If you intend to master the art of success you must understand that with effort comes skill, therefore skillful results appear to come effortlessly. The person who is successful in his or her craft appears to demonstrate the craft with effortless ease. This ease is apparent to anyone watching. What is not so apparent is the years of dedicated practice that comes before what you are seeing. If you would like a great example of this for yourself watch a master violinist play. Then pick up a violin yourself and try to get it to make even one decent note. The master makes it look effortless.

It is not the strength of men,
But the duration, of great sentiments
That makes great men.

—Friedrich Wilhelm Nietsche

If you are working to perfect a craft at this time, no matter what it is, know that if you continue to polish you craft, one day it will come to you mindlessly. Then, those watching you will be astounded by the ease with which you demonstrate your craft. This is the ultimate compliment; someone watching you, thinking that your craft is effortlessly displayed. The master understands this well, the student does not. Anything that you look at, that appears simple to do takes time to master, if it is worth your while; you will strive to achieve it. The craftsman is perfecting his craft every time he works, as is the doctor, lawyer or pottery maker. A craft takes a lifetime to perfect. The work is never complete until the craftsman dies.

Quality is not an act.
It is a habit.

—Aristotle

Lesson 77

The 80—20 Rule Priorities

This is a simple principle. 20 percent of what you do accounts for 80 percent of your results. That means that you are not using 80 percent of your time and skills. How many times do you spend countless hours to make something just that much better? The warrior must know the limits. Exceeding them causes waste, and that is something that the warrior can not have. It ties directly into the over-do-it principle, which so many people follow here in the US. You may have heard it more often than you remember; if two aspirin cures your headache, then four should cure it faster. Or if I eat half the calories I should lose twice as much weight. These are common misconceptions. The skillful strategist understands that everything needs to be kept in moderation. In order to keep things in moderation, the warrior is in a constant battle to understand the limitations.

Look at the next project you undertake. How important is it that everything go off without a hitch? Is it worth wasting 80% of your time on it? Can you spend 80% more time in order to make sure it is one hundred percent? Remember that even if you are spending this extra time there could still be a hitch. But if the hitch then pops up, you are demolished. Prepare yourself for any adverse outcome that could happen, then go with what you've got. If the world waited until the airplane was perfect, we might still not have commercial air travel.

Imagine if the salesman were to actually spend 100% of his time selling. Instead he spends much of his time gathering leads, learning about his product, driving to a location or waiting for a prospect. Bear in mind that the 20% of the time you are engaged in your "actual duty" you must make it count, and make it count with 100% dedication. There is a point at which you will reach the point of diminishing returns. Be aware of this point and bear it constantly in mind.

Focus your energy and time on that which is most beneficial in achieving your goal.

Lesson 78

Understanding the Self by Listening to Others

Honest criticism is hard to take,
Particularly from a friend, an acquaintance, or a stranger.
—Franklin P. Jones

Listening to other people's criticisms about you will teach you more than their compliments will. When I was training to attain my teachers' credentials, I often had the opportunity to study under some of the top instructors in the world. I would ask each and everyone I met what mistakes they saw me make. If any compliments came my way I would accept them gratefully but then quickly move back to the criticisms. I noted that the more criticisms that I could hear, the more I could overcome, the less would exist in the future.

Too often we look for compliments because compliments soothe our soul. By focusing on them we ignore our own opportunity for growth. It is by understanding our weaknesses that we build upon our strengths. The constructive criticisms we receive give us the opportunity for bettering ourselves. Within them lie the answers we seek for extended growth. The compliments keep us exactly where we currently are. Those who look for and accept criticism well grow at a much more rapid rate than the person who looks only for compliments does.

Often people "Shoot the Messenger". That is why I tell you to learn to distinguish between the bearer of bad news and the bad news itself. Often the person who brings you the bad news may only be telling you something that could benefit you. The news that is brought to you may or may not upset you. But by "shooting the messenger" you are cutting off the tip of the weed, the root, or problem that lies underneath still exists, it will eventually grow back. Look at the problem and examine it carefully. Ask questions and use the messenger as the tool. Ask these questions:

Is this a situation that is a problem with the messenger himself or is he acting as the go-between?

Are there any suggestions or possible fixes that the messenger is telling me that I can use to rectify the problem?

How long has the problem been as issue?

Why is he / she telling me this?

Why is he / she telling me this right now?

Remember that everything that happens, happens for a reason at a given time—-there are no coincidences. When you receive this message, you are at a *cosmic-ready* time to accept the lesson. Even though all the chips might be down and this seems to be the end-all bad news, it is the right time. Trust in yourself, trust the message and trust that the answer will come to you. It is your duty to find the answer. The answer will lead you to enlightenment.

I would like to remind you of an old Chinese proverb to bear in mind if you are ever the giver of criticism:

> *Do not use a hatchet*
> *To remove a fly from your friend's forehead.*
> —*Chinese proverb*

Lesson 79

Self-Amazement is Self-Defeating

Conceit is G-d's gift to little men.

—*Bruce Barton*

I often see fighters who are so impressed with themselves that it leaves little room for anyone else to be impressed by them. The true warrior wins without fanfare or hoopla. His victories are void of ego and show.

As a warrior it is important to learn not to make a show out of your personal accomplishments, no matter how great or grand. If you want others to be impressed by you, win them over with a humble attitude. Any time you make a show of something you did, it weakens the significance of what you accomplished to others. Allow the people who watch you to comment on your greatness. Accept praise modestly and move on.

The humble warrior wins not only the battle but also the approval of others.

In the same tone it is important not to make a spectacle at the expense of someone else. In the warriors' days even the death of the person you battled had to be done with respect. In a sword battle the kill had to be clean and direct. If a person were to commit Seppuku (ritual suicide), many times another person stood by to ensure that it would go without a hitch. If the person could not follow through with it, the observer's responsibility was to finish the job. Honor was, and still must, be of primary importance in all areas of our lives.

In Judaism this principle goes as far as the meat observant Jews eat. Among other practices, the animal to be slaughtered must be killed in a single blow, if not; it is not considered kosher and cannot be consumed by observant Jews. The respect for the animal goes before the will to eat of the people. The animal in many *Earth religions* is held sacred. Thanks are given to the Creator for the food as well as to the animal for its sacrifice in feeding us. True respect transcends people, it goes to every living and inanimate object. True respect is the respect within us.

If you are a boss or supervisor, degrading someone in front of his or her peers is useless. The person will grow to resent you and that hostility will demolish the morale that is necessary for the growth of the company. Even if others agree that the person was wrong, they will fear that one-day they may be subject to a similar spectacle. No one respects a person who does not respect others. If a person respects himself, he will respect others.

Lesson 80

Holding on to Something that Harbors Negativity is Negative

To be wronged is nothing
Unless you continue to remember it.

—*Confucius*

Warriors may sometimes appear cold and cut off. On the contrary, the warrior understands the need to sometimes let go. If you are involved in something that is damaging to you emotionally, you need to let it go. More often than anything this will involve a person. You are sad to let go and let this person out of your life, but deep down in your heart you need to, you must. The pain that surrounds having the person there is demolishing the person you could be.

To break the bridges that bind us is the only way we can grow. Look at your own personal relationships. How many of your friends are constantly telling you, you cannot do something. That your dreams are just that, dreams. If it is negative, and I mean truly negative, you have to get it out of your life, once and for all. You need to understand the difference between negativity and criticisms. When someone criticizes you, it is more than likely to help you and teach you to grow. The person who puts you down is doing just that, putting you down. To determine the difference, ask yourself the following questions.

Is there some truth to what he or she is saying?

Does this person offer me a possible solution?

Does this person genuinely care about me?

Have they shown that they care about me in the past?

What does this person have to gain by my failure?

What does this person have to gain by my success?

Is this person offering advice or help through this process?

In answering these questions honestly you can better understand where this person is coming from. If they come from a negative place, understand this and understand that they are the ones in need of help. If not, look to them for the help they can offer you.

Lesson 81

The Warrior Works for Himself Even if He is Under Another's Employ

Many people grudgingly go to work each day miserable that they are not their own boss. They skate by doing just what needs to be done to finish off the day. They await the lunch bell from the moment they arrive in the morning, and then they watch the clock for 5:00pm to roll around so they can go home. Sadly enough, they take this attitude in almost everything they do. Their energy is low and their attitude is negative. Chances are they will have this attitude until the day they die unless they learn otherwise.

No matter what it is you are doing, do it with 100% vigor and with all of your heart. When you eat, eat with all you have. When you rest, rest completely. If your job doesn't suit you, do it 100% until you find a job that suits you better. Taking a despondent attitude toward any one thing will adversely affect you in many other areas of your life.

If you work for someone, the best attitude to take is that the business is yours and that you are a partner. You must make yourself so valuable to your employer that the business can not run without you. It reminds me of a story of the famous Hollywood power broker Michael Ovitz, a true warrior. He worked at The William Morris Agency in the mailroom. But, when many of his co-workers went home at 6:00pm he stayed. He would walk the floors of the building, read about the clients, the company, future projects: he would educate himself in the agency business. He was a warrior; he took on the agency to be his. He confronted the president of the agency one-day and told him, "I have some ideas that could make our agency better." Imagine a guy from the mailroom telling a senior executive how to run a business. How would you imagine the executive reacted? Michael Ovitz became an agent faster than anyone else ever had at The William Morris Agency. Michael carried this vigor throughout his tenure at the agency then sprang off to open his own little agency. Many laughed at him. How could he challenge the big agencies in Hollywood? Simple, hard work, and a total belief in what he was doing. He surrounded himself with people who were like-minded. Each of these people took the attitude that the agency was theirs. The result? Creative Artists Agency in the 80's and 90's was the premier power broker in Hollywood. With a phone call, Michael Ovitz could make or break a career. He became Hollywood's premier power broker by employing the warrior mentality.

Belief in yourself and in what you are doing never fails. You might give up before it works, but don't mistake that with failure. If you follow through over and over, you cannot fail. You have to keep your mind focused on the goal and see the outcome.

Commitment unlocks the doors of imagination,
Allows vision,
And gives us the right stuff to turn our dreams into reality.
—*James Womack*

Lesson 82

One Day the Hunter Will Become the Hunted

On teaching some of my students the concept of attacking and counter-attacking, a good question arose. The student pondered, "If I lift my sword above my head to attack, can't my opponent sneak in and attack my midsection?" YES! They were starting to understand. I was ecstatic at this moment. Why? Because they were starting to grasp that attacking is stepping outside of the balance of nature. It is wrong.

How can we use this principle in business? Simple: The rule of silence. In negotiating, silence is such an important element. Often to say nothing is to win.

When a prospect brings up objections, list them. Get all of them. Look at the list and say to your prospect, "Are these the *only* reasons you are not ready to buy?" It is your goal to get the person to agree with you here. Overcome these objections. After overcoming the last objection, you must insert the close. "So Mr. Prospect, I know the most important reason you'll want to do this today is _____ (insert your counter to their strongest objection here—I like to save this one for last). Then place the agreement in front of them and say nothing. Silence will be your best friend at this point.

To open oneself up for growth we open ourselves up for failure.

To open ourselves up for joy, we open ourselves up for sorrow.

To open ourselves up for financial gain, we open ourselves up for financial failure.

To open ourselves up for love, we open ourselves up for pain.

Often through pain, suffering and adversity we experience growth.

In order to enjoy the extremes, we may also have to experience their adverse side effects.

Lesson 83

Think Like No One Else

Where there is no vision,
The people will perish.

—*Proverbs 29:18*

Once in a great while a person comes around who thinks like no one else. Most of the time these people are dismissed as lunatics, or outcasts from society. Their opinions are only heard by a very few. But the people who believe in them are steadfast in their belief. You need to think like no one else. If someone thinks something can't be done, and you believe it can, believe it 100%. That will convince the others to believe in you as well. Even if they don't, it won't matter, you will prove otherwise. Stripping yourself of limitations, having an open mind and clarity of thought will move you above all others who move with the masses. Thinking like everyone else, not believing in miracles, being pessimistic and all the other qualities that make up the masses is unattractive. It is the people who stand out that excel. If you keep your expectations there where everyone else's are, you are condemned to stay right there where they are. Your results will be the same as theirs. Elevate your thinking to a higher plane. Look for the opportunities where other can't see them. This comes through self-mastery. Only the person who is so secure with himself, with his convictions and his opinions will be able to sway the consensus.

Once you elevate your thinking above all others, you will gain superior results.

If you think this sounds far fetched, I would like to give you some examples of people that were viewed as outcasts by the masses during their times because of their way of thinking. Understand that they were excepted by some, but as a whole the masses did not accept their ways of thinking or acting.

Some of these people are:

Jesus, Moses, Ghandi, Martin Luther, Dr. Martin Luther King Jr., Albert Einstein, Henry Ford, and the list could go on endlessly. Each of these people believed 100% in their convictions. Several gave their lives for their beliefs. Are your beliefs strong enough where you would give your life for them? How strongly do you believe? Think about this, the stronger you believe the stronger your conviction will appear to others.

A man is what he thinks about all day long.
—*Ralph Waldo Emerson*

Lesson 84

Adding Time to Your Day

If you want to achieve mastery, you need to dedicate time to better yourself, either through education or other forms of self-improvement. Imagine if you could study a language or a craft for one hour a day how much progress you would make at the end of one-year. The trouble is, adding the time into your day. Most people feel they can't squeeze another minute out of the day. This is primarily due to either poor time management or lack of priorities. How much time is wasted watching television, driving to work, talking needlessly on the phone? How could you change this and use this time for self-improvement? Here are some ideas:

While driving to and from work, listen to foreign language tapes or self-help tapes instead of music on the radio.

While you're watching television do some exercises or stretching.

When you are sitting idle read a book.

On the weekends attend a course.

Wake up 30 minutes early to spend time on a correspondence course.

Consolidate your phone call list to only important ones.

Schedule a business meeting at lunch; kill two birds with one stone.

Carpool with co-workers and plan your meetings in the car.

There are countless ways to make more out of your day. When I go to sleep, I always try to listen to a good self-help book on tape. It subliminally trains my mind to think sharp. Even if I don't remember exactly what I heard, my subconscious does.

The more you can do in your down time, the more benefits you will reap from your up time.

Lesson 85

Who's Talking—
Who's Listening

Small people monopolize the talking.
Powerful people monopolize the listening.

Write these words down and study them well, students of **the craft of the warrior. He who speaks least, says the most.** Many masters I have trained with have turned my entire training around with the subtle nod of their head. The inferior teachers have spent countless hours explaining the hows and whys. The person asking the questions controls the conversation. The person answering is merely being led.

The warrior prods his opponent to see what position he'll take, then the master moves in for the kill. The more information you can garner on the person you are dealing with, the better your position will be. The only way you will find out about him/her is to ask questions and then listen carefully. Never interrupt or interject. Listen   Listen   Listen. The key to success is to hear what the other person says and be able to understand what they mean by that.

If you are in sales and ask the right questions, you will know the objections the consumer has before they even come to his mind. You'll be able to overcome these objections in a matter of fact form.

Customers like to deal with a salesperson that listens to them. This way they feel they are not being sold, they feel they are being helped. Being a good listener involves letting go of the self. Ego is the number one adversary standing between good listeners and loudmouths. He who has the ego will feel constantly compelled to explain why he or his product is the best, why his service will outperform his competitors. The warrior addresses none of these issues. The warrior instead addresses the issue of "How does my product/service best serve the customers needs."

People who ask questions are seen as people who are sincerely interested in other people.
And as we all know, we like people who are interested in us.

It's better to keep one's mouth shut and be thought a fool
Than to open it and resolve all doubt.
—Abraham Lincoln
…men of few words are the best men…
—William Shakespeare

Lesson 86

Viewing Everything You Do as Important

That many people are frustrated with their current place in life is no secret. But, on the bright side, everyone who is frustrated has an opportunity that the President of the US does not. Let's say you were the president of the United States. You have a job for four years, maybe eight, then… nothing. Where do you go from there? Everything else from there is really downhill. Even running General Motors is a big step down from running the entire nation. So you, in your temporary place right now, you have the brightest outlook of all. The lower you are the brighter the outlook. You have so much room for improvement, so many chances and opportunities that the ex-president does not have.

Miyamoto Musashi said it best when he said: "Do nothing negligently." Approach everything you do as important. Many people think that only the job above theirs is important. By constantly daydreaming about "how great it would be if only I had my bosses job" will never get you there. Making your current place the most important thing in your life will.

Everything everyone does is important. Keep this in mind constantly. The janitor is as important to GE as the vice president. Empires are rooted from the ground up. The person who lays the bricks for the building is equally as important as the architect who designed the structure. There is little hierarchy when you cut down to the bare bones of it. Look at your job as the all-important assignment it is. Do your best at it and give it all you have. Once you conquer it, you will move up the ladder until you're on top. The person who gets to the top of the ladder from the first rung up understands what is underneath him far better than the person who jumped onto it from another ladder.

Immense power is acquired by assuring yourself in your secret reveries
That you were born to control affairs.

—Andrew Carnegie

Lesson 87

The Virtue of Sincerity

Because of *non-judgmental openness* the warrior is a master of sincerity. He does not falsely flatter or shower a person with idle gifts. The warrior also does not tolerate these things done onto him.

When you deal with others, deal with them as you wish to be dealt with. Someone constantly showering you with false flattery is insulting. Better to pick one quality that is sincerely admired and focus on that rather than make up 50 others. This is seen as vane. If a compliment is not given in a sincere fashion, it is an insult, because the person did not spend enough effort to search out the true characteristic of the person. When I compliment someone on something, I look deeply for something that the person may hold dear to himself or herself. Perhaps a characteristic that is important to them and was important to them to have achieved. For example, whenever I hear that a person is making a conscious effort to better their health through diet, not smoking or drinking, exercise or meditation, I tell them how much I admire their self-will and mental fortitude. Then I discuss that with them. Why? because that is something that I too am sincerely interested in. It shows the person that I care and I will talk to them at length about it.

Sincere interest outweighs false flattery.

The warrior is a master of sincerity. He will engage in conversation with anyone. He knows that he can learn and gain from anyone he meets. He will take a very sincere interest in what others have to say, listen carefully and respond sincerely. Useless conversation on the other hand is a waste of time for the warrior. He wishes to gain by his endeavors, he wishes to help others succeed. Everything he does is geared at sincerity and success.

In your day to day interaction with others see if you can put this principle to work. Work hard to pick out a quality in someone that sincerely interests you, then expound on that. Do not blindly compliment someone in order to hear yourself talk. Sincerity, sincerity, sincerity...

A wise man will be master of his mind
A fool will be its slave.

— *Publilius Syrus*

Lesson 88

Become A Master At Interacting With Others

In order to master the art of success you must understand what is best for you. Once you understand this, you must be able to make it beneficial everyone else. Use the benefits and gains you receive from your own success to help others. By so doing, your success will not be rooted in selfishness or negative self-interest.

If you are trying to achieve something, look at the opportunities your success can create for others. If you rise to the top of your department, how will you make life better, more prosperous, easier, etc. for others in your department as well as throughout your organization. Focus on the big picture. If you can make your thoughts known, then do so. Tell others what your goal is and why. What will you add, what will you change. Keep your goals tied to that that can be achieved in a realistic period of time. No one wants to hear a pile of promises and be met with a heap of letdowns later. If your goals are pure, people will believe in you. Now, instead of you pulling for yourself, you've just employed an army.

People who look to succeed not only for their own best interest, but also for the good of others, will always have an easier time prospering.

Selfish goals lead to eventual self-destruction. Employ your goals for the good of your fellow man. Then your goals as well as those of your fellow as will be rewarded.

Whatever it is that you wish to achieve is possible. You must not be content with anything less. Your destiny lies in your hands. Use it for goodness or evil, the choice is up to you. The evil will lead to self-destruction eventually. Goodness flourishes. Go for the goal and go for the good. Don't settle for less than first place. Remember that second place is just first among the losers.

Those who accept mediocrity are condemned by it forever.

Lesson 89

The Most Powerful Muscle Is The Mind...

The mind is its own place
and in itself can make a heaven of hell or a hell of heaven.
—*Milton*

If you can only grasp one thought, one excerpt, one lesson from this book or any other book on self-help in the world, this should be it. The place you are, is the place you make. A person working in the mailroom of a big accounting firm can look at his situation as dismal, being at the bottom of the ladder of his company or he can see it as an opportunity for growth. What a better place to be working, learning all the ground floor lessons that make the company tick. In fact the person in the mailroom probably has more information at his fingertips than half the executives upstairs. Looking at this position as an opportunity for self-growth gives you a springboard for success. Learn from where you are now, and remember these lessons. The person who remembers the lessons they learned on the way up, is less likely to face them on their way down, if they in fact ever do come down. Furthermore, the respect that one gets from working their way to the top of the ladder is far greater than that which is given to the person born with a silver spoon in their mouth.

Thinking positive thoughts leads to positive results. The mailroom clerk who faces his day-today responsibility with a positive mental attitude and sets his goals on success will on day be an executive. Just as the executive with a negative attitude will one-day fall from power.

Positive mental attitude is the single most important characteristic for success. As a warrior in the battlefield you must imagine yourself slaying your opponent before your sword ever leaves your scabbard. So be it in your daily chores. If you are an executive you must picture your company at the top of the ladder on a daily basis. Utilizing a positive mental attitude with creative visualization will give you the tools to prosper. You can not be held back if you are succeeding in your own mind.

Lesson 90

On Looking Ahead

For many years I have studied the atrocities that have occurred during the Holocaust. How could this happen and why? I have been blessed in my life to meet survivors who lived to tell. I have met several, and read about countless others. What made them tick? What did these *survivors* have that some of the others may have lacked? What went through their minds? I have read many of their accounts, and on several points they were quite similar. When asked, "What helped you survive in the day to day?" many of them answered, that *one day they would stand in front of others and tell about their trials and tribulations*. I must add at this point that so many countless died without a chance of survival. The people of whom I speak here are the ones who were malnourished, punished, and riddled with disease. The ones who were killed had no chance of survival. The ones with strong minds simply had the mental fortitude and were able to overcome these secondary killers which existed.

In their minds they were already seeing another light. One great survivor was Simon Weisenthal, he not only survived the concentration camps, not only lived to tell about it, but also lived to become the most successful Nazi hunter ever. Once the prisoner, now the prison keeper. Did he run? No. To this day, the great Mr. Weisenthal lives in his home country of Austria. Fear did not move him. This was his home. In his book, *Justice not Vengeance,* he talks about his philosophy. He wanted to bring these people to trial, not assassinate them in the street, although the same respect was not shown to the victims in the 1930's and 1940's. It is Simon Weisenthal's plan to follow the path of the just.

Think of how we can learn about overcoming any adversity we may face in our daily lives by learning from the lessons of these people. To understand that one day we may speak to others about our problems should give us the fortitude to persevere. If I am at the bottom of the ladder now, I know that by successful thinking, I will have an interesting story to tell when I am at the top of the ladder.

Many times I have delivered speeches telling of myself as a frail young boy who was beaten-up almost daily in elementary school. Now I stand 6'2" and weigh 190lbs, I have attained a seventh degree black belt and travel over the world to instruct individuals as well as government people in the art of hand-to-hand combat. I too had a picture in my mind that I would one-day talk about these problems. I found those answer at a young age, perhaps ten or eleven. I didn't learn this from a self-help book, instead it was taught to me be a great teacher—my mother.

Experience cold or heat,
Pleasure or pain.
These experiences are fleeting;
They come and go.
Bear them patiently.

—Bhagavad Gita

Lesson 91

The Three Tools For Success

There are three tools that will help you achieve more. They are as follows:

A sincere desire to do more. A sincere desire is more than a mere thought or idea that you may want to do something. You must crave more than what you now have. You wish for bigger and better things in order to better your life and the life of those around you. With every sincere desire there is a motivation, a reason for the desire. The motivation/reason differentiates a whim from a desire.

The intelligence to select a tool to realize that desire. By intelligence I do not necessarily mean the knowledge to meet the goal, but instead the intelligence to seek out the proper person or tool to do it. Henry Ford himself did not build the V8, but he had the intelligence to surround himself with the people who could do it.

Perseverance to see that desire through. Undying perseverance. No matter how many no's you meet along the way keep looking for the yes. Even though others may think you foolish in your persistence, you'll know better.

How many of these tools are in your tool cabinet? I bet more than you think. Since you have made the decision to read this book, you have already accomplished two of the criteria: You have a sincere desire to learn, and you have the intelligence to select a tool to realize that desire. Perseverance is however the most important, and that is up to you!

You will need to continue through up times and down times. Continuing positive attitude training must be a priority in your life. Just like the person who gets into a fitness routine and diets to get into shape must continue these regiments forever, not just stop when they arrive at their goal. By stopping once you attain a goal, you will instantly begin moving backwards again. When other things pull your attention off the path, you need to get right back onto the path and continue. The person who does not allow their distractions to keep them off the path is the person who will succeed. Please note that I said, "*keep them off of their path*". This is important to note. Many people will be distracted. Many times throughout my training I have become distracted. I simply took the time to deal with the distraction and then got right back onto the path. Don't just ignore distractions or sweep them under the rug. They will only grow bigger and come back to haunt you. Deal with them now, while they are still small. The faster and better you deal with them now, the better armed you will be for your future battles.

The secret of success in life is for a man to be ready for his opportunity
When it comes.

—*Benjamin Disraeli*

Lesson 92

If You Stumble, Remember The Five Characteristics

*Write these words down on a piece of paper or
an index card and look at them everyday:
Ambition, Initiative, Belief, Desire & Perseverance*

Along the road of success you will undoubtedly meet obstacles. In fact you should worry if you don't meet any obstacles at all. The warrior of success is able to overcome the obstacles with his or her arsenal of weapons. Knowledge is the most powerful weapon any warrior possesses. If you could break down your knowledge of overcoming obstacles it could be summed up in the following five characteristics. When you are confronted with a new goal or desire, or the one you face is giving you a struggle, check off which of the following characteristics you may be currently lacking. There can be no struggle or lack of success if all five of these are present.

Ambition sparks the need for what you want to attempt.

Initiative gives you the fuel to start that challenge

Belief re-instills your fuel when the chips are down

Desire keeps you on the track

Perseverance doesn't let you stop no matter what the obstacle.

There can be no weakness if you do not lack any of these characteristics; you are on the road to success. Anyone can lack one of these at any time. The person who finds themselves in trouble is the one who thinks he can ignore the lack there of. When you see you are becoming weak, re-empower yourself. Just as if you are thirsty you must drink. These five elements are the staple of success. Address your weakness and re-empower yourself. You'll be right back on track.

> *Only he who does nothing*
> *Makes no mistakes.*
>
> —*Anonymous*

Lesson 93

You Can Have Anything You Want...

I read a book that said these lines and I thought it was brilliant. Now let me finish the sentence. **You can have anything in life you want, but you can't have everything you want.** Think about the brilliance of this statement. Simply put; prioritize what it is that you want. Be sure to think about what it is that you want and then go get it. If you want to be a successful actor, but on the way to realizing that goal somebody offers you a job as a cameraman, you have to pass. If you want to be a family man and somebody offers you a million dollar a year job on the road, you have to pass. The master warrior is not distracted by what may sound good at the moment. He looks to what it is that he wants and what he has set his goals to be and continues to pursue that. It is this that he bears constantly in mind. He is not easily distracted, offers that come in from the side are merely flies that he brushes away.

As any good teacher will tell you, write down your priorities. Keep a list. Look at that list often and bear it constantly in mind. Look at the top item on the list. It should be so important to you that all the other goals should end up on page two. Your number one goal is what you need to bear in mind day and night. It may take you several months or a year to decide what it is that that goal is. When you find it, and are certain about it, it should become your life goal.

Mother Theresa set her goal on helping the children, she did just that. She wasn't distracted by anything. Even when the Pope would stand next to her, the children were still her priority. She was a warrior of the highest caliber.

Now for the second part, ...but you can't have everything you want. There lies an important lesson here for everybody. You may end up banging your head against the wall if you try to get everything you want. Set your priorities and be ready to accept the trade-off. No matter how successful you become, there is no way of having everything that you want. You may not realize this until it is too late, that is why I would like to forewarn you. While working as a bodyguard I met many people whose life-goal it was to be famous. They thought they would never be sick of throngs of adoring fans loving them. On the contrary, many times they wished only for anonymity. Be careful what you wish for, you may just get it. Be persistent in your desire- then be content with your accomplishment.

> *First say to yourself what you would be,*
> *And then do what you have to do.*
>
> —*Epictetus*
>
> *Aim at nothing and you'll succeed.*
>
> —*Anonymous*

Lesson 94

A Warrior's Tool For Dealing With Negativity

Seven times fall down,
Eight times get up.

—Japanese proverb

Yes, even warriors get down. The trick the warrior has learned is how to get back up again. Negativity is so powerful that it can demolish even the strongest man or woman. If you took one drop of negativity and put it in a positive pool, the pool would no longer be positive. By the same token, if you put positive into a negative pool, negativity would still be there. To overcome the negative energy, overflow the positive. If something is slightly negative blast it out with 200 times the positive energy. If your pool has two gallons of negativity in it, drop 100 gallons of positive into it. You can't put too much positive in. The negativity must be eradicated so that it understands that it can not come back, ever.

If the negativity comes in the form of a disappointment, pick yourself up and brush yourself off. Whatever it is, deal with it and move on to the positive things that make you happy. Maybe you need to treat yourself to a weekend away, a massage, a lavish dinner or something else. Immediately take the negative energy that has arisen and flush it out with feelings of happiness. Sometimes a walk eases the mind, exercise, a movie or just chatting with a friend. Wallowing in the negativity only gives it the opportunity for growth. In order to eliminate it, you must shift your focus onto the happier, more positive aspects of your life. My mom used to tell me when I became frustrated in my endeavors:

If at first you don't succeed, try and try again.

I thought the irony of this so great. What my mom told me as a little boy, I would be blessed to tell people in my career.

Lesson 95

A Picture Is Worth

It's not what you believe,
It's what others receive of what you believe...

I'm sitting on a beautiful mountaintop, the air is clear and the sky is blue with a few big puffy white clouds. The grass is lush green and the trees are so tall they almost touch the sky. The stream that flows next to me is dowsed with giant rocks that redirect the flow of the crystal clear water.

Where did your mind go for those past few sentences? I'm sure to the stream or my mountain top setting. Although we as humans communicate with words, we perceive in pictures. Think about this as a skill in communication. The reason you were able to see the stream and the mountain and the sky is because I saw it when I wrote the words. I was there in my mind, and was as a result, able to take you there too. Instead of pitching an idea in numbers and figures, do it in terms of landscapes and benefits. The car is not a hunk of steel with tires. It is a safe vehicle, with a ride like a chariot that will take you and the family on a drive through the hills comfortably and safely. While you are snuggled in the comfort of the plush seats cradling your body like a feather pillow. Think of the advertising that Michelin uses. Michelin is not selling tires, the are selling the child sitting in the tire, the safety that this tire provides to the child.

You can apply the picture book principle to whatever you are selling. Think in terms of benefits and relate them to a picture that you would paint if the person who you are speaking to could not understand the language. Explain in vivid details, become an artist. Selling by the use of a visual medium is the easiest way to get on the same side as a client. He doesn't care about the details; he wants to know about the benefits. Benefits sell.

The moment of enlightenment is when a person's dreams of possibilities
Become images of possibilities

—Vic Braden

Lesson 96

As You Think So You Are

Some powerful words to think about. That which we think in our minds we can become. Which explains why so many people are broke, because they tell themselves over and over again that they can't get out of debt, chances are they never will. Get off of the negativity wagon.

One of the worst results of negativity is "emotionally induced illness". How many times do you hear somebody saying, "I feel run down", "My lower back is killing me"? Not to soon after they end up with a cold or a wrenched back. If only they would fool themselves into the contrary. On countless occasions I have played this trick on myself, and it has worked. 90% of the students of my dojo came down with a flu bug that was going around several years ago. I refused to let it get to me. I did sneeze a few times and felt warm, but I never addressed it. When people would ask me if I had the flu yet, I always said no, I feel great. I was not sick one day that year.

Confidence will win over pessimism. Some students of mine were playing with a pistol crossbow that I had at the school. They took it outside to try it out. They set up a target about 50 or so feet away. They tried and tried and couldn't hit it. A couple of them were quite accomplished with a bow and arrow as well as with firearms. In fact, they were convinced that it was absolutely impossible to aim this flimsy

$10.00 contraption this far. I watched and smiled. They asked if I thought if I could do any better? I said, "*Of course, I'm a warrior.*" I took the crossbow, extended my left arm (although I'm right handed), lowered it toward the target and squeezed. When they walked up to the target they found the arrow dead in the middle of it. They stated, "Bet you can't do that again." I explained to them that there was no need to do it again, I had already accomplished my goal. I walked away, and later was told about the discussion that went on after I left. It wasn't my techniques that made the arrow go into the target, it was my confidence. Strengthen your confidence in what you do and say, and you will change the outcome of your life.

> *Man can only receive*
> *What he sees himself receiving.*
> —*Florence Scovel Shinn*

Lesson 97

Fear

A man's doubts and fears are his worst enemies.
—William Wrigley Jr.

Fear exists only in the mind. The body can not understand fear without the mind processing it first. To prove this look at children, the smaller they are, the less they fear. A large dog is just like a big stuffed toy to them, a razor sharp knife is just a shiny plaything, and the list can go on. Any fear you feel is a result of having learned something about possible failure. The only reason I wouldn't skydive is because I think there is a possibility that the parachute might not open. The only reason most people don't want to stand in front of an audience is they feel they might look stupid, or not know what to say, or what they say may not seem important.

You need to address the fears in your life, at least those that you can conquer without risking your life. That's why I won't tell you here to overcome you fear of jumping out of airplanes. If you fear speaking to people, practice in front of a few of your friends. A good way to start is to learn a good joke and then tell it. Chances are you'll beat the fear quickly. Fear of public speaking is among the greatest fears that people possess. So chances are if you can lick that one, the others won't be that hard to beat. Remember that in public speaking all eyes are focused on you. These people are here to see you and hear what you have to say. You are already in their eyes established as a knowledgeable, reputable person. When I speak to an audience I always remind myself of this. These people came here to see me, I'll give them all I've got. That's all I can do. That is what they should expect, and that is what they will get. I know I'll give them my best, I know that's what they want. Therefore, I have no reason to be nervous, I'm only delivering a product to them.

All fears can be overcome. The only fear you need to keep constantly in mind as a warrior is the fear of death, this one you can't escape. Eventually we all will die. If you keep this fear in mind you will be motivated to constantly strive for more before you "run out of time". Be ambitious in your endeavors and start them today. Keep in mind the fear of death. The longer you wait to start, the less time you'll have to finish.

Confidence is acquired and developed, few if any of us are born with it. Action cures fear. Once you begin doing that which causes you fear it will become familiar to you. Once it is familiar to you, you are less likely to fear it.

Fear makes the wolf bigger than he actually is.
—*German proverb*

Lesson 98

Spiritual Suicide

Happiness is the meaning and the purpose of life,
The whole aim and end of human existence.

—Aristotle

Although many of us have never considered suicide we commit mental and spiritual suicide every day. Physical suicide is usually a quick painless way to end suffering and escape problems and pain. Spiritual suicide is a slow, degrading process that tears away at our will. Therefore spiritual suicide is generally the precursor to physical suicide. Even if physical suicide does not follow, the suffering continues. We need to address the counter-action to spiritual suicide.

The subconscious has two safes. Each safe holds the experiences and lessons of our lives. Each time we experience something, a memory thereof is deposited into the safe. Now, when a new opportunity presents itself, we weigh the options against our past experiences. If the good outweighs the bad, chances are it's a go. If, however, we look at the negative side of all of our experiences, then we probably won't be doing much in the future. If the job we *lost* becomes the deposit instead of the new higher paying job we *gained*, then the deposit is a *negative* one. If the relationship that failed is the deposit instead of the opportunity for growth, again it's a negative deposit.

We need to get into the habit of going to the positive safe for withdrawals. This will beneficially enrich our lives. We will see that even in failure lies opportunity. And with opportunity there is hope.

> *We all live with the objective of being happy;*
> *Our lives are all different and yet the same.*
>
> —*Anne Frank*

Lesson 99

The Warrior Seeks Out The Silver Lining

Where others see failure, the warrior sees opportunity. When others think the chips are down, the warrior sees an opportunity to pick them up. It is much easier to be optimistic than pessimistic. Optimism holds hope and opportunity, pessimism yields only failure and despair.

My dad once told me that G-d doesn't close a door where He doesn't open a window. Opportunity is all around us. Seek opportunity out. Through belief and conviction practice the following exercise:

Turn impossibilities into probabilities,

Probables into possibles,

And, possibles into definites.

The key way to do this is by eliminating one word from your vocabulary, that word is *impossible*. There is nothing in the world that is impossible. Whenever you come up with something that is impossible, there is someone somewhere that will want to prove you wrong. Look at your job. What is impossible that you can attempt? What will you have to do to make it possible? Hire an assistant, change your work schedule? More than likely, the first thing you'll have to do is change your attitude. Because as long as you believe something is impossible, it will always be impossible to you.

Remember, how you think determines how you act
How you act in turn determines how others react to you.

By keeping a positive outlook, others will see you as an optimistic person with a great attitude. People react better to positive people than to those who are always down. No one would trust their stock portfolio to a broker who is down in the dumps because the market is down 500 points. They would however trust the broker who sees this downfall as the greatest opportunity to buy the deals of the century. Remind yourself often of positive qualities; look for them in everything you do. Opportunity abounds if you'll only look for it.

We must look for the opportunity in every difficulty
Instead of being paralyzed at the thought of the difficulty in every opportunity.

—Walter E. Cole

A man who has made a mistake
And doesn't correct it
Is making another mistake.

—Confucius

Summary

I hope that the lessons in this book have helped you to better understand the attainment of your own success. It is important to remember that success lies within you. No one who achieves anything is successful unless they first recognize his or her own success. Once you begin "successful thinking" and applying the techniques in this book you will be more than half way there.

The overall goal of success should be happiness. And, happiness is something that requires absolutely nothing. I have been happy listening to music and dancing around my apartment unemployed, almost as often as I have enjoyed happiness as the result of a large commission check. *Happiness is making the most of what you have and who you are.* Understand this and the world is your oyster.

The master of success is the person who does not give up when he or she believes that their goal cannot be met. As a warrior you must understand that you should welcome the troubles you meet along the path because they are the lessons that will make you stronger.

One of the biggest secrets to creating success and happiness is to try and make others' lives better. When our efforts can help someone who may not be able to help him or herself, happiness and success are certain to abound. Always try to be certain that what it is you wish for does not violate anyone else, be certain that what is best for you is also good for others.

I wish you well on your path to success and I promise that if you follow these simple rules you are certain to arrive there.

Thank you for reading my book,

Robert Cabral
www.robertcabral.com

About the Author

Robert Cabral is best known as a martial art master, he holds senior masters' credentials in traditional Karate-do. He is the producer and host of "Be Your Own Bodyguard" a series of self-defense DVD's for men and women. He is a true Renaissance Man. He is an accomplished photographer, author, speaker, TV personality and success coach. He has educated, inspired, motivated and entertained thousands throughout the US and Europe. He is fluent in English, German and Swiss German. His philosophy is deeply rooted in the Eastern and Western principles of the ancient masters. He is a passionate student of life and has studied philosophy and religion and is currently working on a film about religion.

Robert is very passionate about animal rights. He is an animal lover and hopes one day to open a sanctuary for animals. He currently lives in Malibu California with his dog and parrot. In his spare time he enjoys songwriting and playing guitar.

0-595-18401-4

www.ingramcontent.com/pod-product-compliance
Lightning Source LLC
Chambersburg PA
CBHW061350280526
45784CB00001B/202